WHAT DIFFERENCE
COULD A REVOLUTION MAKE?

WHAT DIFFERENCE COULD A REVOLUTION MAKE?

Food and Farming in the New Nicaragua

By Joseph Collins,
with Frances Moore Lappé and Nick Allen

Food First

Institute for Food and Development Policy
1885 Mission St., San Francisco, CA 94103 USA

Library of Congress Catalog Card Number: 82-21032
ISBN: 0-935028-10-2

Printed in the United States of America
1 2 3 4 5 6 7 8 9

To order additional copies of this book, please call or write:

Institute for Food and Development Policy
1885 Mission St.
San Francisco, CA 94103 USA
(415) 864-8555

Please add 15 percent for postage and handling ($1 minimum).
Bulk discounts available.

Distributed in the United Kingdom by:

Third World Publications
151 Stratford Rd.
Birmingham B11 1RD
England

Library of Congress Cataloging in Publication Data

Collins, Joseph, 1945–
    What difference could a revolution make?

    Bibliography: p.
      1. Agriculture—Economic aspects—Nicaragua.
2. Land tenure—Nicaragua.   3. Land reform—Nicaragua.
4. Food supply—Nicaragua.   I. Lappé, Frances Moore.
II. Allen, Nick, 1950– . III. Title.
HD1817.C64   1983   338.1'097285   82-21032
ISBN 0-935028-10-2

Design: Kerry Tremain
Type: G & S Typesetters, Austin
Printers: McNaughton & Gunn, Ann Arbor
Text: Goudy Old Style
Display: Goudy Old Style Bold

TABLE OF CONTENTS

LIST OF TABLES AND CHARTS

Acknowledgements

I AM GREATLY INDEBTED TO THE SANDINISTA government for the unwavering trust in me they have demonstrated over the past three years. Even after I told them I had decided to write about my experiences, they never showed the slightest hesitation about making themselves and their internal research—as well as the Nicaraguan countryside—available to me. Their candor is exceptional for government officials anywhere. At the same time they have never tried to control or even monitor what I was writing.

Special thanks must go to Jaime Wheelock, Minister of Agricultural Development and Agrarian Reform; Salvador Mayorga, Director General of the Agrarian Reform; and numerous other officials of the ministry, especially Roberto Gutierrez, Pedro Blandon, Alvaro Reyes, and Ivan Garcia.

Also, I wish to acknowledge the invaluable cooperation of CIERA, the Nicaraguan government's agrarian reform research center. So many there have been helpful for so long that I hesitate to name anyone in particular for inevitably I will leave some out who deserve to be thanked by name. But I am deeply indebted to a CIERA staff member and old friend, Peter Marchetti, S.J., who remained always ready to help right up until the final fact-checking phone call. I would like also to thank CIERA director Orlando Nuñez S. and staff members Pascal Serres, Michel Merlet, Peter Utting, David Kaimowitz, and Eduardo Baumeister.

I am also indebted to many other institutions and individuals in Nicaragua, notably Xabier Gorostiaga, S.J., the Ministry of Planning, the Instituto Historico Centroamericano, the ATC, the UNAG, Sean Swezey, INIES, John Weeks, Elizabeth Dore, and hundreds of campesinos and farm workers who have so forthrightly told me what they think. Also Felipe Paz, Margaret Randall, the Maryknoll Sisters, the Jesuit Fathers, residents of Ciudad Sandino and several other barrios, Peter Shiras, Arnold Weissberg, Matilde Zimmerman and Tommie Sue Montgomery.

Thanks also to those living outside Nicaragua whose writing has been so useful: Solon Barraclough, E. V. K. Fitzgerald, Joseph Thome, Jacques Chonchol, David Baytleman, Eugene Havens, Carmen Diana Deere, Philippe Bourgois, Jaime Biderman, Valerie Landau, Gustavo Esteva, Larry Simon and Michael Scott of Oxfam America, Alejandro Schetmann and George Black. While I have greatly benefited from their willingness to share their work, they are without responsibility for the use I have made of it.

This book would not have been possible without the Institute for Food and Development Policy. Therefore I want to thank the several thousands Friends of the Institute (see coupon at end of book) whose small contributions make the Institute possible, as well as the foundations and individuals who have helped us. In particular, I wish to express our appreciation for the J. Roderick MacArthur Foundation, whose support for this project was vital to its completion. Frances Moore Lappé and Nick Allen provided invaluable conceptual and editorial help. I also want to single out Institute colleagues past and present: Michael Morrissey, Steve Goldfield, Philip Russell, JoNina Abron, Sharon Huff, Nancy Guinn, Gretta Goldenman, Jennifer Lovejoy, and Debbie Fox. Thanks also to Cindy Crowner of NICA.

Every time I attempt to write the acknowledgements for a new book I admonish myself for not keeping a notebook noting those who help as the project goes along. Once again, I have failed. My omission is compounded by the fact that this book has been a three-year effort and there are so many to thank, so many whom I will recall only after this page goes to press. To all of them, my gratitude and my apologies.

Joseph Collins

ONE

"NICARAGUA IS A SCHOOL"

IN AUGUST 1979, THE INSTITUTE FOR FOOD AND Development Policy received a long distance call from Managua. On the other end of the line was an official in Nicaragua's Ministry of Planning. He asked for Joe Collins. "We are putting together an advisory panel of people with experience in problems of agrarian reform and food policy. Would you be willing to come down for a working session to discuss Nicaragua's policies? An international church group will pay your way."

That was the beginning of my unique opportunity to learn firsthand about the process of change set off by the Sandinista-led popular insurrection which had overthrown the Somoza dictatorship just a month earlier. During the three years since that phone call, I have visited Nicaragua ten times as an unpaid advisor on food and farming policies. In late 1981, Institute cofounder Frances Moore Lappé, editor Nick Allen, and I began working together to analyze the changes underway in the Nicaraguan countryside as well as in the national food situation. This book is the result.

The more we learned about Nicaragua, the more we felt Americans were being deprived of an opportunity to see Nicaragua through the eyes of Nicaraguans themselves. So in early 1982 Frances and I went to Nicaragua together, interviewing Nicaraguans in all walks of life. This collaboration resulted in our book *Now We Can Speak: A Journey Through the New Nicaragua*, a companion to this one.

We've entitled this opening chapter "Nicaragua is a school" for several reasons. First, you hear often hear this phrase—"Nicaragua es una escuela"—from Nicaraguans because it describes how they feel about the process of change they're engaged in. For us, it has a special meaning.

For many years we have sought to understand the roots of hunger throughout the world. Through our work at the Institute for Food and Development Policy we've learned that a society's food and farming policies are a powerful lens through which to evaluate the priorities, sympathies, values and effectiveness of any country's leadership. This is especially true in most third world countries which, like Nicaragua, are overwhelmingly agricultural.

In this book we will ask you to join us in seeing Nicaragua through "food glasses." Doing so makes it possible to see behind the newspaper accounts which too often transmit only the U.S. government's one-dimensional portrayal of Nicaragua's geopolitical role in the East-West conflict. Focusing on food and farming, we are able to report more broadly on how the lives of the Nicaraguan people are being affected by the country's new economic and social policies.

What has struck us about Nicaragua's new leadership is its clear common purpose: to build a new country based on what many Nicaraguans call "the logic of the majority." For too long, they believe, Nicaragua has operated according to the "logic of the minority," meaning that decisions were made in the interests of, and usually by, the wealthiest 10 percent of the population. As a consequence, the majority of Nicaraguans had been made among the poorest people in Latin America. The incidence of malnutrition had doubled in the ten years before 1975, crippling the lives of almost 60 percent of children under four years of age. By the time of the insurrection, 60 percent of rural people had been deprived of land they needed to feed themselves. Just 1 percent of landowners—a mere 1,600 people—had usurped almost half the land.

The success of the war against the dictatorship and the disintegration of the old system of exploitation, the new gov-

ernment argues, means that now the needs of the majority—
Nicaragua's poor—should come first. But while the "logic of
the majority" provides a direction to guide the country's new
leadership, it does not tell them which road to take or which
vehicles are best suited for the trip. That they must learn by
analyzing their experiences as they go along and by studying
the experiences of other peoples.

The Nicaraguan leadership confronts seemingly impossible
tradeoffs as well as many unknowns and unforeseen consequences in pursuing policies guided by the "logic of the majority." Nowhere is this more true than in food and farming.

The first tradeoff is obvious: By definition, redistribution
of privately owned land means that some will gain, while
others—the minority who control most of the land—will
lose. Inevitably, those who have to give up some of their land
will not be happy.

But the tradeoff is more complex than simply trading the
privileges of the rich for the rights of the poor. While the
"logic of the majority" might superficially be interpreted as
requiring the expropriation and rapid subdivision of big estates, the Nicaraguan leadership has not seen it that way. If
export crop production on the large estates were undermined, the entire society—of which the poor are the majority—would suffer. So the Sandinista leadership has resisted
the redistribution of any land that is being used productively.

For this reason a sense of justice, as well as a desire to respond to the demands of the landless, has had to be traded
off against the need to keep up production of export crops,
essential to obtain the foreign currency necessary to import
what Nicaragua can't produce itself.

A related tradeoff confronted the Sandinistas. If they responded to the demands of the poor for land to grow their
own food, then how would they be able to attract enough
workers to help harvest the export crops? After all, when
people can feed themselves from their own land, what's to
assure that they'll still be willing to do the back-breaking
work of picking cotton for 10 hours a day?

How have the Nicaraguans wrestled with such painful
tradeoffs? This question, which has intrigued us for the last
three years, is at the heart of this book.

While we have been intrigued, we have also been impressed. In three years we have witnessed this Pennsylvania-size nation of 2.5 million people make remarkable advances, especially remarkable because they have been achieved at a time when conditions of life are worsening in most other countries in Central America and the rest of the third world.

Since the beginning of Nicaragua's revolution:

—Over 40,000 landless rural families have received access to land on which to grow food for the first time.

—Production of basic food crops—corn, beans, rice, sorghum—is up. Land grants to the rural poor, lowered land rents, generous government farm credit and better prices have enabled poor farmers to increase their production of the country's food staples. Corn and bean production have climbed 10 and 45 percent respectively, while rice production has doubled compared to 1977-78 (a representative Somoza year).

—Export crop production is also up—coffee by 10 and sugar by 20 percent compared to 1977-78.

—Consumption of basic foods has soared. Corn consumption is up by a third, beans by 40 percent, and rice by 30 percent since 1978, the last year before the war.

—Food self-sufficiency is at hand. Following excellent 1982 harvests, imports of major staples have either been eliminated or substantially reduced. Nicaragua will soon be exporting rice and possibly beans.

—Infant death has been reduced. The infant mortality rate, perhaps the best measure of family nutrition and availability of health services for the poor, has been cut by one third. An anti-malaria campaign has reduced the incidence of malaria by 50 percent. Over one million Nicaraguans have been vaccinated against polio, measles and tetanus, diseases which continue to kill millions of people throughout the third world.

—Illiteracy has been dramatically reduced. A volunteer-based national campaign has cut illiteracy from over half the population to less than one-seventh. Over one million Nicaraguans—40 percent of the entire population—are involved in some kind of formal schooling. Over 1,200 new schools have been constructed, 95 percent in the countryside.

We have focused on these achievements because, since most did not require huge sums of money, they could in theory be accomplished in other third world countries where control over economic resources in a few hands has impoverished the majority. That they were achieved in Nicaragua testifies to two things. First, the value of basing government policy on the "logic of the majority." Second, the broad support for the new government's policies, especially among the poor rural majority. This support is evident not only in widespread voluntary participation but also in the initiative of tens of thousands of Nicaraguans without which many of these advances would have been impossible. These gains become even more impressive in light of the multiple obstacles we discuss below.

What Makes Nicaragua Different?

The Sandinistas' ability to grapple with seemingly impossible tradeoffs, to learn from previous revolutions, and to stay on course in the face of threats from its more powerful neighbors, especially the United States, shows they are different from many other revolutionary movements. What makes Nicaragua different? And what can we learn?

To begin to answer these questions, let's return to the beginning, to my invitation to help advise the men and women formulating Nicaragua's food and farming policies. Among those invited to join the informal advisory group were people who had participated in developing agrarian reform in both the Christian Democrat and Popular Unity governments in Chile, those with expertise in food and farming in postcolonial Africa, and others like me who had been studying agrarian reform in many different societies. The very fact that Nicaragua's new leaders chose to gather such advisory panels—not only for food and farming but also for education, health, etc.—tells something about their openness.

Working in Nicaragua has given me a close-up look at

other qualities of Nicaragua's young new leaders. First of all, I have learned, they are serious people! Our meetings often began early in the morning and lasted late into the night. The Nicaraguans did not ask the foreigners what to do. Nor did they tell us what they were going to do and lobby for an endorsement. Rather, they often presented us "experts" with a number of options along with the relevant data (such as it was). They wanted those more experienced than they to help shine a light down the road each policy might take their country. What are the consequences which we might not foresee, they asked us.

In itself, this approach told us a lot. It revealed qualities which we have come to recognize again and again in our dealings with Nicaraguan leaders. They do not tend to be doctrinaire. They do not attempt to plug in rigid, preconceived, ideological formulas. They continue to adapt their policies in light of their experiences.

In working with the leaders in the agrarian reform, I have witnessed a genuine humility rooted in honesty. Over and over again, I've heard them admit, "we just don't know the answer"—or say, "yes, we've made a mistake."

I've also come to appreciate their pragmatism. Very realistically, the Nicaraguans concluded that their shortage of experienced leaders meant they had to rely on the knowledge and help of others. It also meant working toward a policy they call "national unity," that is, trying to maintain support for a program of reconstruction among both the capitalist producers and the peasants. *Business Latin America*, a weekly for managers of multinational corporations, summed up a recent survey of Nicaragua: "Despite increasing reports of bitter conflict between the Sandinista government and the private sector in Nicaragua, the great majority of international companies surveyed by BLA describe their relations with the government as good, or at least reasonable. . . . 'People in the Ministry of Economy are pragmatic,' one executive explained."

Another striking feature of the Nicaraguan revolution is the extent of voluntary initiative. While I was in Managua in February 1982, for example, 70,000 volunteers were giving up a Sunday to participate in a polio vaccination campaign. The Sandinistas' approach to controlling malaria, a disease of epidemic proportions in Nicaragua, reveals the unique potential of voluntary initiative. Instead of spraying DDT in an effort to kill the mosquito vectors, they opted for the safer and ultimately more effective *simultaneous* vaccination of the *entire* population, thereby eradicating the problem essentially by ensuring humans would no longer be carriers. While public health authorities have long thought this method superior, it requires mobilizing virtually the entire population in one mass effort. Nicaragua is one of the few countries that felt capable of this massive effort.

Mass participation in large part accounts for the success of the insurrection itself. By 1978, the year before victory, an overwhelming majority of the Nicaraguan people, from all walks of life, were directly or indirectly supporting the Sandinista-led struggle to topple Somoza and his National Guard. During the final insurrection against the dictatorship, Sandinista leaders admitted that spontaneous uprisings of the people took the initiative away from the leadership.

The motivation of so many of its leaders also distinguishes the Nicaraguan revolution. Motivations, of course, are difficult to assess, but what struck me as I talked with people throughout the country was the deeply religious purpose which so many expressed. Innumerable government and peasant leaders have described to me how their commitment was sparked in Catholic study groups where, as teenagers, they met with friends to discuss the Bible and reflect on the relevancy of Jesus' teachings in a society of gross injustice and misery. Moved by these reflections, some went to live and work among the poor.

These religious teachings stressed the innate value of each human being and, from this, the individual's right to control the resources he or she needs to live with dignity. The grounding influence of Christianity is reflected in many of the decisions made since victory. "Implacable in combat, generous in victory" has been a slogan of the Sandinista-led government from the start. The Sandinistas stand out for their lack of vengeance against their enemies. Immediately upon victory the government abolished the death penalty and went to great lengths to insure legal trials for all of the captured National Guardsmen accused of crimes. (Much to the outrage of many Nicaraguans, whose loved ones had been murdered by the Guard, the government released half of the original 8,000 Guardsmen captured for lack of sufficient individual evidence against them.)

Respect for the individual is also reflected in the Sandinistas' flexible economic policies, allowing people to choose what will work for them. Farm cooperatives, for example, are totally voluntary, although the government encourages them through credit and services where they appear to be economically appropriate. Indeed, in the countryside I've found dozens of varieties of cooperatives because the members in each place decided what would be best for them.

The Nicaraguan revolution also stands out for the extraordinary participation of women. During the fighting women worked in supportive functions, as combatants and even as military commanders; by the time of victory about 30 percent of the Sandinista forces were women. (In Margaret Randall's moving book *Sandino's Daughters*, Nicaraguan women tell what these new roles meant to them.) Today women have important roles in government and in the mass organizations. The Nicaraguan revolution is also fostering the flowering of distinctly Nicaraguan culture in a country long considered a subsidiary of the United States. The first-ever Festival of Campesino Music brought national attention to previously obscure villages. And building on the national indignation at the U.S. government's wheat cut-off, the Nicaraguans organized corn festivals—including dances and imaginative cooking contests—to stimulate the pride of the people in their indigenous grain. Ninety new theatrical groups have sprung up as well as at least two dozen community centers offering workshops in painting, poetry, drama, music and dance. Over a hundred poetry workshops supported by the Ministry of Culture are awakening creative expression in the slums, the factories, the army, the prisons, and even the police. For the first time, Nicaragua has a film institute—not just serving the city-dwellers but bringing film by mule and backpack into even the remotest villages.

Finally, the Nicaraguan revolution does not use a cult of personality to glue the new society together. There is no Nicaraguan Mao or Fidel, and the leadership appears intent on making a common vision, not a personality, the binding force. Leadership is a collective undertaking: the three-person Junta works closely with the nine-person National Directorate. The only personalities promoted as national symbols are the revolution's martyrs, especially Augusto César Sandino, who fought the U.S. Marines in Nicaragua in the 1920s and 1930s and was assassinated by the first Somoza in 1933. (The Sandinista Front for National Liberation, or FSLN, took its name from Sandino.)

A Common Legacy of Underdevelopment

While the Nicaraguan revolution is uniquely Nicaraguan, the country shares a common history with other under-developed countries whose economic and human development has been distorted by decades of external and internal exploitation.

That legacy involves not only the concentration of land and wealth in a few hands but also its fruits:

—Good land underused, and the best land used not for food for local people but for luxury export crops to further enrich the already wealthy elite.

—Extraordinary dependence on, and therefore susceptibility to, the international market. If any one of Nicaragua's four major export crops drops a few cents a pound on the London commodity markets, the country's entire economy can be undermined.

—No experience in democratic process. Indeed, 45 years of ironclad dictatorship taught Nicaraguans that to speak out was to risk your life.

This legacy of underdevelopment results in innumerable surprises that can undermine even the best-intended policy, as the Nicaraguans have learned. So abysmal, for example, was the collection of national land tenure statistics under the Somoza dictatorship that the new leadership didn't even know how much land the government confiscated when Somoza and his allies fled the country. In the first months, they thought they had up to 60 percent of the land, which they could make available to Nicaragua's poor. But when the dust settled, they ended up with just over 20 percent—one-third what they had expected.

Similarly, agricultural planners have been frustrated by the virtual absence of good roads in much of the country's food-growing regions. Thus, while peasants used the government's generous new farm credits to produce more rice and beans, much of the food never got to the markets. There was simply no way to transport it.

These are just two of the twists that have deepened our understanding of the difficulties of building a more just society out of the ruins of an extremely unjust and inefficient one.

Not the least of the legacy of underdevelopment is the dearth of experienced leaders, technicians and managers. Over and over again we have been struck by the youth of those who now must shoulder enormous responsibility. Nicaraguans in their twenties and early thirties, many with no administrative experience whatsoever, have taken charge of entire ministries of government.

Driving from the airport into Managua, Nicaragua's capital, the shells of bombed-out factories have continually reminded me that on top of the legacy of underdevelopment is the devastation of war. In Nicaragua this, too, is extreme because Somoza ordered the National Guard to bomb and pillage his own people to punish them for their impudence. About 50,000 Nicaraguans were killed and another 100,000 wounded, out of a total population of 2.5 million.

This costly war and Somoza's personal greed drained the country. The destruction of the war, capital flight, and the debt inherited from Somoza came to $4.1 billion, according to a U.N. study. The foreign debt alone, much of it incurred to line the dictator's secret foreign bank accounts and to purchase arms, stood at a crushing $1.6 billion. In 1982, Nicaragua pays out 52 cents of every dollar earned from its exports just in interest and on repayment of its foreign debt.

As if all this were not enough, Nicaragua also confronts the economic crisis hitting all Central America. Prices for the country's basic exports have fallen while the prices of needed imports have risen. Of Nicaragua's export earnings, 40 percent goes for petroleum imports. In 1977, Nicaragua had to export 4.4 tons of coffee to import a tractor; only four years later, the same tractor cost the equivalent of 11.2 tons of coffee. By 1982, the price of sugar, another major export of the region, had fallen to the lowest level in ten years.

Not surprisingly, then, only two countries in Central America showed any overall economic progress in 1981. Nicaragua, in spite of these monumental obstacles, was one of them. Indeed, significant advances in Nicaragua's food production stand in sharp contrast to Costa Rica's food crisis. By mid-1982, Costa Ricans were crossing into Nicaragua to buy beans and rice.

Lessons from Nicaragua

As a student of the causes and proposed remedies of world hunger for many years, the theme of my work at the Institute for Food and Development Policy can be summed up in one sentence: hunger can only be eliminated through political and economic changes that redistribute power over food-producing resources. In 1977 Frances Moore Lappé and I completed the first edition of *Food First: Beyond the Myth of Scarcity* (Ballantine revised, 1979). Since *Food First* is more an analysis of the roots of hunger than a blueprint for change, we are often asked: How could any poor country, given the incredible legacy of underdevelopment, even begin to attack the roots of needless hunger? So naturally we sit up and take notice when a government claims—as does the Nicaraguan government—to be working to end hunger. Indeed, we take special note of Nicaragua because, before the overthrow of the dictatorship, most Nicaraguans had been made among the poorest people in Latin America, despite the agricultural wealth of their country.

But we have learned to be leery of governments' claims of concern for their poor. We've watched governments in India, Brazil, the Philippines and other countries, claiming to be concerned about the hungry, launch costly aid-financed programs to increase food production. But despite production successes, hunger has deepened precisely because such governments repress movements for change which would redistribute power over basic resources, allowing people to feed themselves. We've watched other countries, some calling themselves "socialist," sacrifice the well-being of the rural poor for the sake of urban industrialization.

Of course no one can predict the future for Nicaragua. But I have been grateful for the opportunity to take this intimate look at a country attempting to put "food first." My perspective has always been critical, analyzing the high hopes and good intentions along with the mixed reality. But what has struck me over the last three years is the consistent and staggering discrepancy between my perspective, based on close contacts with Nicaraguans from all walks of life, and the one presented by the the Reagan administration and the mass media in the United States.

Whatever happens in Nicaragua, Nicaragua *is* a school. Even if Nicaragua's leadership should become a new unaccountable elite, we would still have much to learn. We would have to learn *why* the country moved in this direction. We would have to ask what role the United States played in forcing Nicaragua to reduce political and economic pluralism.

Dismissing such an outcome as inevitable is too easy— and, I believe, profoundly wrong. First, it assumes that there is nothing we can do to stop our government's apparent attempt to make life in Nicaragua as difficult and repressive as possible. Second, it discounts the genuinely democratic spirit of participation we have witnessed in so many Nicaraguans. From my experience, I feel certain that Nicaraguans want to learn from the mistakes of previous revolutions, not repeat them.

TWO

IMAGINE YOU WERE A NICARAGUAN . . .

THIS BOOK IS A STORY OF A SOCIETY STRUG-gling to remake itself. It is a story of sacrifices, compromises, achievements, disappointments, fears and hopes. It is a story of people willing to risk their lives for change.

To understand why so many Nicaraguans have been willing to risk their lives for change, we must try to imagine ourselves as typical Nicaraguans before the overthrow of the Somoza dictatorship.

Imagine it's 1977 and you are a 17-year-old Nicaraguan. Your family, like two-thirds of all rural families, has either no land at all or not enough to feed itself. If yours is "lucky" enough to have a little plot of land, half or even more of what you grow—or a steep cash rent—goes to the land-owner in the city.

Last year you watched helpless as your little sister became repeatedly ill with diarrhea. Your parents saw her losing her strength but there was no one to help. In all of rural Nicaragua there are only five clinics with beds. The first few times your sister pulled through. But by then she was so weak that when measles hit, you watched her die after four painful days. The year before your brother died right after birth; your mother and father have lost five of their children.

You cannot remember a day when your mother was not

worried about having enough food for your family—and, of course, you never really did have enough or your little sister wouldn't have died from measles. You heard once on a neighbor's radio that Nicaragua was importing more and more corn, beans, and sorghum. And you've heard about the incredible *supermercados* in Managua. But without money you can't buy food no matter how much there is.

The seven people in your family share a single-room shack, divided by a thin partition. The floor is dirt, there is no electric light, no toilet, no clean drinking water. You are outraged when you hear Somoza boast to some American reporters that "Nicaragua has no housing problem because of its wonderful climate."

You hardly know anyone who can read and write—except the priest, of course, but he's from Spain. You'd like to learn but there is no school. Anyway, you must work.

To buy a few simple tools, some cooking oil, sugar, salt, and kerosene, your father has to borrow money. But the only source of credit is the the local moneylender who makes him pay back half again as much and sometimes much more. Not surprisingly, your family is forever in debt.

Locked in debt and without land to grow enough food, your family is forced to labor on the coffee, cotton, or sugar estates. But such work is available only three to four months a year at harvest time. Since the pay is miserable everyone in your family must work to try to bring in enough: your mother, your grandmother, your older sister—about 40 percent of the coffee and cotton cutters are women—and your father and brother. You had to start picking coffee when you were six. For filling a 20-pound bucket you earn only 16 cents. Working sunup to sundown, you might earn a dollar.

Your "home" during the harvest is a long, windowless barrack built out of unpainted planks or plywood. With the other exhausted workers—men and women, old people and children, sick and well—you sleep on plywood slabs, called "drawers" because they are stacked four or five high with only a foot and a half of space between them. There is no privacy for there are no partitions. There is no flooring, no windows, not a single light bulb. The only toilet is the bushes. Filth all the day long. For three to four months a year this is home for you and for over 400,000 other Nicaraguans.

Working on the coffee estates is bad, but picking cotton is even worse. You found that out one year when your family had to travel even further, down to the Pacific coastal cotton estates, to find work. At least coffee grows in the cooler regions. But on the coastal lowlands the blinding tropical sun hangs in a cloudless sky, bringing temperatures to well over 100 degrees. You had nothing to protect you from the cotton branches, the pesticide-saturated fields, and the maddening swirl of gnats and jiggers.

Placing your baby sister on the edge of the hot, dusty field, your mother picked cotton as fast as she could, filling her sack and rushing to the weighing station so she could hurry back to nurse. She didn't know that tests would probably have shown that her breast milk had over 500 times the DDT considered safe for consumption by the World Health Organization, a frightening contamination due to twenty to forty aerial DDT sprayings a year of the cotton fields.

In the harvests, too, hunger is a constant companion. All you get are small portions of beans and fried bananas and, rarely, some rice or corn tortillas or a bit of smoked cheese in place of the bananas. Yet for this food, about three hours' wages are deducted from your pay. Even here, you're sure the owner makes profits. You only see meat on the final day of the harvest when the patron and his family put on a "feast."

As you grow older, you realize that even though your family has no land, it is not because your country lacks land. You learn—quite likely through a Catholic priest—that there are more than five agricultural acres for every Nicaraguan, and potentially twice that. The problem is that most of the land is owned by the few big landowners. The richest 2 percent own over 50 percent of the land, while the poorest 70 percent of landowners—and that doesn't include your father, who only rents his miserable plot—own only 2 percent of the land.

Not only do the rich own most of the land, you discover, but clearly they've got the best land. Their soil is most fertile and flat. Yet they waste its potential, using it mostly to graze cattle. By the 1970s, in fact, 10 out of 11 million acres used for export production were being devoted to cattle grazing. While you are constantly hungry, you discover that 22 times more land goes to produce for export than to grow food for Nicaraguans. And much of the food-growing land is so poor and hilly that it should be in pasture.

While you are growing up your grandmother tells you stories of how things got to be the way they are now, stories she heard from her parents back in the 1880s.

In those days, the powerful people had large cattle haciendas, but they were less concerned about producing beef and milk than they were in just holding on to the land. For many who traced their descent from the *conquistadores*, land was the primary source of their status.

Because they needed few workers, these land barons were content to let people like your great-grandparents work parcels of land, although, of course, they never got legal papers for it. So, while your great-grandparents were poor campesinos, at least they could feed themselves from their small farm, called a *chacra*. They grew corn, beans, and some vegetables, had some banana and other fruit trees, and kept a few pigs and chickens.

Then, somewhat before your grandmother was born—in the 1870s and 1880s—the Nicaraguan countryside began to change rapidly.

The demand for coffee in foreign countries was booming and Nicaragua's landowning elite, as well as new immigrant investors, were quick to respond. With visions of coffee trees as money trees, they broke up scores of cattle ranches, planting pastures with coffee trees.

To give a law-and-order veneer to pushing your great-grandparents and tens of thousands of campesino families like them off their *chacras*, the coffee entrepreneurs pushed through a "Law of Agrarian Reform" and other legislation. It put up for auction indigenous people's communal lands and much of public and church land. Although your great-grandfather and other campesinos had worked the land for years, they stood no chance of getting it. They were easily outbid by the coffee interests.

When the poor refused to get off the land they had worked for decades, the new owners drove cattle onto the *chacras* to trample and eat the crops. Your great-grandfather was almost killed in 1881 when thousands of dispossessed campesinos rebelled. Five thousand were massacred.

The new coffee barons needed not only land but labor, especially at harvest time. Robbing your great-grandparents of their self-sufficient farms insured that they would have to go to work on the big estates. How else could your great-grandparent's family survive? And as if necessity were not enough, laws were decreed requiring campesinos to show proof on demand that they were employed during the coffee harvest.

To survive between harvests, your great-grandparents migrated toward the central part of the country, the "agricultural frontier." There a cattle rancher allowed them to slash and burn some virgin land in order to plant corn and beans. But once they had their first crop or so, the owner put cattle on the land, telling your great-grandparents they'd have to clear more land if they wanted to eat. It was in one of those clearings, your grandmother tells you, that she was born.

You understand now that the history of your family, like tens of thousands of Nicaraguan campesino families, is tied to coffee. But you wonder where all the endless fields of cotton came from.

Your father explains that while he heard some talk of cotton when he was a boy, it was only in 1950, just ten years before you were born, that "white gold fever" hit Nicaragua. In only a few years the white puff balls took over the Pacific plain as far as you could see, north to south and right up to the base of the volcanos. The cotton plants wouldn't hold down the rich volcanic soils and soon the region became plagued with dust storms.

By the mid-1950s, cotton topped coffee as Nicaragua's biggest export. Somoza saw to it that the cotton investors got cheap bank credit, for he personally reaped millions of dollars on the cottom boom. It's completely unfair, your father tells you, that the rich export farmers don't even risk their money; he and the other campesinos grow what people really need most—basic foods—yet they can't get even the smallest bank loan.

In the cotton bonanza, campesinos, most of whom did not have any papers for their lands, were bought out for next to nothing; failing that, they were forced off the land. Absentee landowners returned to evict their campesino tenants and rent out their lands to cotton entrepreneurs.

When campesinos resisted, the National Guard burned

their homes and crops and pulled up the fences. Indeed, some of the cotton speculators themselves were high officers in Somoza's National Guard, Nicaragua's army and police set up by the U.S. Marines. You understand more than ever why your father and all his friends hate the Guard.

Cotton took over the land that had been growing corn and beans, rice and sorghum, all the basic food crops of the people. The tens of thousands of displaced peasant producers at best wound up as sharecroppers and cash renters on plots of earth too small and poor to support them.

Some of the campesinos run off the land by the cotton invasion pushed east and north into the "agricultural frontier." There, just like your great-grandparents had done, they cleared trees and brush on the huge cattle haciendas only to be forced onto new uncleared land by cattlemen seeking to cash in on the next export boom—the 1960s boom in beef exports to the United States.

Pushed even deeper into the mountainous interior, these tens of thousands of campesinos are even poorer than your family. Almost half the year they are entirely cut off from the rest of the country: even a burro can't get through the muddy trails and dirt roads. Few have ever seen a doctor, even though the area teems with disease, including malaria and adult measles.

You think about all of this—what the priest says, your sisters and brothers needlessly dying, the stories of your grandmother and of your father, and what Somoza claims—every time you look down from your family's little hillside cornfield at the cattle grazing on the fertile valley plains of Somoza's lawyer.

*

Okay. Now it's 1980. You are yourself again, not a Nicaraguan. Maybe you are an American and this morning you pick up the newspaper and find a big story on poor peasants "invading" some farmland in Nicaragua. Your knee-jerk reaction might be—oh, those poor peasants have been stirred up by the revolutionaries who just took over Nicaragua. The revolutionaries are fueling hatred against all the landlords just to make themselves more popular. Those landowners *own* the land. They have legal title. The law has to be respected or it will lead to chaos. Not only that, it will destroy production.

But pretending to be a poor Nicaraguan peasant for even a few minutes might, we hope, have tempered that reaction. By helping you see the world through the eyes of the majority of Nicaraguans, we hope to have made a few points very clear, points that you will need to consider as you read the rest of this book. First, there is nothing legal or fair about the landholding patterns that have been created in countries like Nicaragua. As you have seen, it is not the peasants but the wealthy elites who have consistently invaded land by force. Second, there is nothing especially efficient about land ownership concentrated on a few big estates. The land-use patterns that developed in Nicaragua were exactly the opposite of rational, productive use. Third, it doesn't take a band of revolutionaries to show people the deep injustices in their society. The poor generally know the source of their misery. What they lack is the power to change it.

THREE
THE PEASANTS' VICTORY

To UNDERSTAND THE AGRARIAN REFORM UN-
derway in Nicaragua today we have to understand the
impetus behind it—not just the injustice and misery described in the last chapter, but the decades of struggles by the
peasants themselves. In the industrial countries we are taught
such a bleak view of peasants—as ignorant, simpleminded,
and stunted by chronic hunger—that it is hard for us to
imagine them fighting back. So in Nicaragua we sought to
find out to what extent the rural poor were an active force in
giving birth to the revolution.

Fighting Back

As elsewhere in Central America, the Nicaraguan peasants
have not remained passive before the theft of their lands and
the misery of their lives.

No one who wants to understand the Sandinistas in victory can afford to overlook their dependence on the campesinos during the war. From its founding in the early 1960s, the
Sandinista Front for National Liberation (FSLN) worked
with campesinos. What would have happened to the guerrillas pursued by the National Guard without the help of cam-

pesinos who knew the lay of the land? Campesinos fore-warned Sandinistas of the Guard's attacks and provided the guerrillas with food, water, and other vital supplies.

Both campesinos (owners of small plots of land) and land-less agricultural workers joined the guerrillas. One of the ear-liest attacks on the National Guard was carried out by a Sandinista guerrilla column made up totally of small farmers and landless workers under the direction of Colonel Santos Lopez, a campesino who had fought the U.S. Marines with Sandino in the 1920s. Several leading Sandinistas grew up as poor campesinos.

The National Guard's "cleanups"—indiscriminate killings in areas thought to be sympathetic to the Sandinistas—swelled the guerrilla ranks with rural recruits. They sought vindication for years of forced misery as well as for the Guard's murders of relatives and friends.

Many thousands—perhaps more than 10,000—of those who died in the war against the dictatorship were campesi-nos, landless rural laborers, and their families.

Basta! Enough!

In addition to joining the Sandinista forces, peasants ex-pressed their demand for change by seizing plantation land to grow food crops for themselves, as we discuss in chapter nine. By the 1960s, more and more peasants were declaring, "Basta! We've had enough." Even official documents record 240 "land invasions" from 1964 to 1973 just in the provinces of Chinandega and León, where thousand of peasants had been evicted by large cotton planters.

These invasions were met by the armed force of the Na-tional Guard. Despite the violent repression, land seizures picked up after the 1972 earthquake. Using the increased U.S. economic and military aid after the earthquake, the National Guard set up makeshift concentration camps in areas with the most peasant resistance.

Domingo Gomez grew up in a poor campesino family on the east side of Lake Nicaragua, an area dominated by the large Santa Ana hacienda which belonged to a Señor Bon. Shortly after the triumph, at the age of 20, he recounted to me his childhood experiences in taking back land from the big landlords who had usurped it.

Over the years Sr. Bon expanded his hacienda by stealing, with the help of his lawyers and the National Guard, many small staple-food-producing farms to add to his ranch. Tensions ran high for years. Campesinos repeatedly tried to protest to the authorities but no one would even see them. Then in 1976, Domingo, his father, and some other campesinos began to meet at night in the house of the priest, who was active in CEPA. They listened to the Bible and discussed their problems—mainly their hunger and the theft of their land.

One night they made up their minds to act. "We divided up tasks," Domingo explained. "One person would steal wire for fences, another would make posts. The plan was that, working all night, we'd fence off the area we needed for a cooperative before the daylight, before the hacienda knew anything was happening. And we did it." But two days later the Guard came.

"We had only machetes and so we couldn't defend ourselves," Domingo recalled. "The Guard cut the fences and took our animals."

About that time Domingo and a few others made direct contact with the Sandinistas, who helped them plan and gave them some American-made rifles and handguns they had seized from a National Guard stockpile. "The priest was a big help," he explained. "He had a jeep and could hide the arms." Domingo, then 16, joined the Sandinista Front.

"In 1978, we invaded the hacienda, again by night. We put up fences and chopped lots of firewood. The next day we planted our corn. Thanks to the Sandinistas, we were able to defend ourselves. We stayed." (Today Domingo is a national-level leader of the farmworkers' association.)

Cristo, Campesino: The Liberation Message of Christ

But what accounts for the courageous self-assertion demonstrated by many Nicaraguan peasants? Part of the answer can be found in a "subversive" message that began to circulate throughout the countryside in the 1960s. The message: Each human being is important before God and therefore has the right to the resources necessary to live in dignity. This "subversive" message was being spread by none other than the Catholic Church which, next to Somoza, was perhaps the most pervasive force in Nicaragua.

Pope John's Vatican Council (1961–65) helped open the Catholic Church to the daily trials of the world's poor. Then the 1968 Medellin Conference of Latin American Bishops endorsed the reawakening of the liberation imperative within the Christian tradition. Throughout Latin America many bishops, priests, and sisters studying the documents from these historic councils began to seek ways to make the Gospel a living reality for rural people.

In Nicaragua some of the leadership came from the Jesuit Fathers. In 1968, with the support of the Nicaraguan bishops, they created CEPA, the Educational Center for Agrarian Advancement. Initially, CEPA simply trained campesino leaders in appropriate agricultural techniques; but CEPA did this in the context of Biblical reflection. Soon CEPA's work began to embrace the social and political implications of the Christian gospel for those who worked the land. CEPA published *Cristo, Campesino*, a comic book whose recurring message was "You have a right to land." Thousands of copies circulated throughout the countryside.

Another highly significant development during the same period was the Catholic Church's decision to foster a lay ministry. With so few priests, the Catholic Church in Nicaragua had never been able to place many priests in the rural areas. However, with the Vatican Council's emphasis on the priesthood of every Christian, the Nicaraguan Church began to train lay persons to perform many sacramental and other religious functions in rural areas where there were no priests.

These specially trained lay people were called "Delegates of the Word." By 1975, in one remote interior province alone, there were over 900 Delegates working closely with Capuchin Fathers from the United States. The Delegates formed Christian "base communities" in which campesinos and landless workers discussed their problems in light of readings from the Bible. The Delegates were also trained to teach literacy and basic health care. Some Delegates also took part in CEPA training sessions.

CEPA itself, as we have seen, was started basically to teach farm skills so campesinos could better help themselves. No political impact had been intended. Nonetheless, more and more CEPA activists and Delegates came to understand that no matter how hard they worked at it, campesinos could not substantially better their conditions as long as the society was fundamentally structured against their interests. Gradually, the CEPA activists and the Delegates of the Word began to understand that campesinos would have to unite and organize political action. In serving the plantation workers, the Delegates soon concluded that "to hunger and thirst for justice" meant that workers had to organize to demand basic health services, drinking water, liveable wages, and year-round employment.

Early on, the Somoza regime sensed the dangers of a socially interpreted Gospel. The National Guard labeled Delegates of the Word "subversives" and began to harass them. Campesinos disappeared in areas with a strong Delegate presence. Eventually the National Guard repression claimed the lives of Delegates, too, provoking the official church into opposing Somoza.

After 1975, in some northern areas, the National Guard regularly banned all religious meetings. As the repression intensified, many Delegates and Christian base communities were forced to go underground. Instead of quelling the resistance, such repression actually fostered these Christians' collaboration with the Sandinistas.

Many Christians working in CEPA developed into active supporters of the Sandinista National Liberation Front. Several key CEPA activists became directors of the Association of Rural Workers (ATC) which, as we will see, the Sandinistas established in 1977. Some CEPA activists opted to become guerrilla freedom fighters. During 1977–78, at least four CEPA organizers were assassinated by the National Guard.

As the level of CEPA's commitment deepened, the Catholic hierarchy tried to restrict its activities and to discourage it from collaborating with the Sandinistas. Finally, when the bishops left it no other option, CEPA cut its ties with the Church hierarchy and became an independent Christian organization closely allied to the Sandinistas.

Agricultural Workers Organize

Building on the awareness in part created by CEPA and the Delegates of the Word, in 1976 the Sandinistas started to organize Committees of Agricultural Workers, first among the coffee workers in the Carazo and Masaya regions.

Formed on some twenty coffee estates during the harvest period when growers needed workers most, the Committees demanded better working and living conditions. The first confrontations over economic conditions quickly became political, especially because the landowners frequently called in the National Guard, who beat, tortured, murdered, and imprisoned Committee members. It became apparent to all that Somoza stood behind the landowners.

Again the repression backfired. The Committees of Agricultural Workers spread south into the department of Rivas and north to Chinandega, from the coffee estates to cotton and sugar plantations. By late 1977, the northern Pacific zone, completely dominated by cotton and sugar estates, was the most militant area in the country.

Within a year the Committees were strong enough to form a national organization, the Association of Rural Workers (ATC), which united the committees in several departments.

During the export harvest period when seasonal workers were together on the estates and were most in demand, the ATC organized rallies to denounce National Guard repression and demand just wages and working conditions. The Guard responded with tear gas, clubs and even machine guns. ATC members joined anti-Somoza protests in Managua. In the first nationwide work stoppage, in January 1978, they barricaded main roads and cut communication lines in rural areas to protest the assassination of Pedro Joaquin Chamorro, the *La Prensa* editor who opposed Somoza.

In some areas the ATC demanded that large farms be handed over to control by the workers. In April 1978, the ATC published the first issue of its newspaper, *El Machete*.

On April 9, 1978—just a little more than a year before victory—the ATC organized its largest march and hunger strike in the town of Diriamba. The strike was a response to Somoza's callous assertion that the problem in rural areas was not hunger but the lack of a balanced diet! In what has been called its "first baptism of blood," over 1,200 ATC members clashed with the National Guard.

Despite tremendous repression, the hunger strike strengthened the ATC and the resistance. Many of the town's residents threw open their doors to the marchers under tear gas attacks. News of their hunger strike and of the National Guard's violence set off other hunger strikes by student groups, the national women's organization and ATC members throughout the country.

From this point the ATC clearly saw itself united with the Sandinistas in an all-out war against the dictatorship. Often armed only with old hunting rifles and machetes, hundreds of ATC campesinos and farmworkers organized themselves in popular militias. Their courage contributed greatly to the final victory on July 19, 1979.

Taking Back the Land—Even Before the Triumph

The Sandinista agrarian reform actually got under way well before the final victory over Somoza as land takeovers took place throughout the countryside in collaboration with the Sandinistas. They were most common around the Pacific Coast city of León during what turned out to be the final months of the popular insurrection.

For example, La Máquina hacienda, controlled by Somoza's mother's family, lay about a mile outside the city of León. There campesinos accompanied by Sandinista commanders retook the land after the National Guard had retreated, just one month before the final victory. Also in the León area, over one thousand dispossessed campesino families occupied 22,600 acres of Somocista-owned farmland four days before the end of the war and started bringing it back into production.

These land seizures were not only a matter of just vindication (*revindicación*) of the wrongful actions of the bigger landlords. Just as important was the need to provide food in the liberated areas. Working with the Sandinistas, the people of León had liberated their city, Nicaragua's second largest, in June 1979. But no one knew that the war would be over the following month, so food self-sufficiency for the area was top priority. To prevent disruptions in production, the

Sandinistas worked to ensure that farms around León belonging to landowners aiding in the fight against Somoza were *not* taken over. And to ensure future productivity, the Sandinistas also tried to prevent any looting or parceling up of the large, modernized farms seized from the Somocistas. Upon taking back the land, the campesinos and landless farmworkers immediately set to plowing and planting food crops instead of the cotton and pasture grass that had prevailed on most of the farms. With the help of the Sandinistas, the campesinos formed cooperatives to work the land as a team. Some of the largest haciendas were turned into Enterprises of the People (*Empresas del Pueblo*) run by the Sandinista National Liberation Front (FSLN) itself.

Gladys Baez, a 38-year-old woman from the rural areas around León, described to writer Margaret Randall how campesinos took over a Somocista farm during this period: "We knew that whenever there's a war, hunger follows. And if the campesinos can't plan, hunger spreads everywhere. So with the help of Julio Vazquez, an agronomist who volunteered to help us, and a group of campesinos, we made an inventory of everything there was on a ranch in the area. We guarded against the indiscriminate killing of cattle, got people to spare the cows and to eat only what was absolutely necessary. . . . We saw to it that the campesinos had their seed."

Many of us imagine revolution in the countryside to mean peasants' revenge against landlords who have brutalized them for so many years. Even given all our knowledge about the outrages committed against the majority of rural people, we will never fully grasp their rage—rage born of "land stolen, wells poisoned and food crops sprayed with pesticides by the latifundistas," as an ATC leader, himself a farmworker since the age of nine, told me shortly after the triumph. Yet, to a truly remarkable extent, the Sandinista Front succeeded in using its moral authority with the campesinos and landless agricultural workers to restrain their wrath against landowners, including the Somocistas, and to await due process.

Clearly, then, the revolution in Nicaragua was not won by an isolated guerrilla band, acting merely in the name of the people. It was won by a widespread movement with strong bases among the poor majority in the countryside. The revolutionary impetus came from decades of gross injustice; the courage to act, often from the liberation message of the Gospel; the decision to act, from the brutality of Somoza's National Guard.

Rural policies that would be developed during the first post-liberation years were not simply dreamed up by Nicaragua's idealistic new leadership; rather they evolved in large part in response to demands of the peasants and farmworkers themselves. In this book we focus on the Nicaraguan revolution's response to those demands—agrarian reform and new food policies in the interests of the poor majority.

FOUR
NO OWNERSHIP WITHOUT OBLIGATION

"LAND TO WHOMEVER WORKS IT!" WITH THIS slogan, Sandinista leaders undoubtedly assured the campesinos and rural workers that victory against Somoza would mean land for them. After all, Sandino—from whom the Sandinistas took their name and inspiration—had started to implement an agrarian reform program in 1932 by helping campesinos form cooperatives. In their proclamations during the liberation war, the Sandinistas promised agarian reform. The San José Pact, which formally united business people and the Sandinistas in the war, proclaimed agrarian reform a major part of the new Nicaragua.

The Sandinistas kept their word. On the first day after the full triumph over Somoza and his National Guard, Decree No. 3 of the Sandinista-led National Government of Reconstruction authorized the confiscation of all the assets of the Somoza family and its close associates (the "Somocistas"). In one fell swoop, this seventeen-line decree set in motion the nationalization of almost two million acres in approximately 2,000 farms and ranches. Overnight about 20 percent of Nicaragua's agricultural land became part of the "People's Property."

This confiscation decree left a full two-thirds of the farmland in capitalist hands. Here we use "capitalist" to refer to landowners large enough to hire labor or rent out their land, or both. These landowners are different from small farmers ("campesinos") who usually use only family labor. These small producers, unaffected by the confiscation decree, controlled less than 15 percent of the nation's farmland.

Farmworkers around Estelí—an area noted for its courage against Somoza's brutality—told me shortly after victory that they were disappointed that the new government had not expropriated more land. Ill-treated for years by this or that landowner, they were shocked if his land were not taken away.

In late September 1979, a top official of the agrarian reform, Salvador Mayorga, and I paid an unannounced visit to a cattle hacienda near Estelí that had been expropriated because it had belonged to Somoza's lawyer. The workers demanded to know why the adjacent ranch had not also been expropriated. "The owner's a pig (*cochino*)," they complained. "No one wants to work for him." Mayorga's answer—that the owner had not fled the country and was not considered a close ally of the dictator—did not seem all that satisfying to them.

Agrarian reform is a drama that unfolds in response to multiple, often conflicting, pressures on the government— and the Sandinistas seem to understand this well. The only citation from Karl Marx I've seen around the agrarian reform ministry seems to be a favorite of the Sandinistas: "People make their own history, but they do not make it just as they please; they do not make it in circumstances chosen by themselves, but under circumstances directly found, given and transmitted from the past."

So while "Land to whomever works it!" might have been an effective rallying cry during the war of liberation, it got quietly buried once the victorious leadership had to confront the urgent need to get the capitalist farmers and ranchers controlling most of the country's exports back into production. These exports were needed more urgently than ever to import food, medicines, oil, and capital goods into the war-devastated country and to reduce the enormous foreign debt. Moreover, the Sandinistas' choices were limited by Nicaragua's proximity to the likely-to-be-hostile U.S. government. To resist any U.S. destabilization pressures, the Sandinistas

knew they had to do everything within reason to build support among all social classes for the future of the revolution.
"Building the material basis for national unity, not dema-
goguery, is the order of the day," a member of the Sandinista
directorate told me three months after victory.

In this book, we will repeatedly see that the Nicaraguan
agrarian reform is a balancing act. On the one hand are the
pent-up demands from campesinos and landless farmworkers.
On the other are political and economic constraints, not all
of which are readily understood by the rural majority. In
charge of this delicate process the Sandinistas placed one of
the most respected members of the National Directorate of
the Sandinista Front, Jaime Wheelock. When the agricultural development and agrarian reform ministries were combined to form a single ministry (MIDINRA) in late 1979,
Commander Wheelock rose to head the superministry.

Virtually all of the Sandinista leaders are young and inexperienced in government. Wheelock, at 34, was no excep-
tion. He readily admits his own inexperience. "We are mili-
tants in a revolutionary cause who knew little about the
process of an agrarian reform, in theory or in practice,"
Wheelock told a group of us foreign advisors only a few
months after victory. Nevertheless, Wheelock had a special
familiarity with many of the agrarian problems of his country. The son of a well-to-do cotton grower, before the war
Wheelock had written a carefully documented study of the
social and economic impact of Nicaragua's cotton production.

"We are not guided or tied to preconceived models. Our
approach to each problem is very practical," he told Oxfam
America's Larry Simon. "Some people call us Marxists, some
call us Communists, and at the same time others are labeling
us reactionaries, rightists, bourgeois—as happened during
our recent trips to the United States and Colombia. But we
must respond to problems in practical and concrete ways." In
another interview Wheelock stressed, "Just as we made the
revolution a Nicaraguan revolution without copying models,
so we are not going to make an agrarian reform by imitating
other countries. Of course, we do take into account the experiences [of other people]."

The first step in this balancing act, as we have seen, was
the nationalization of all the properties that belonged to

Somoza, his family, his lawyers and other cronies—the So-mocistas. Since most of this land had been abandoned when Somoza and his friends fled the country, the new government's move was not politically difficult. The government did not have to evict landowners. In fact, most members of the landowning class even supported the government's take-over of Somoza's land, for they too had come to despise Somoza at least by the final months of the war. Thus the confiscation of Somoza properties did not ignite any brouhaha over private property rights. In addition, the agrarian reform's birthright came without a price tag: "compensation" to Somocistas was out of the question. Everyone knew much of this land had been stolen in the first place. Indeed, this first step can most accurately be thought of not as agrarian reform but as the confiscation of the property of a handful of criminals.

Uneasy with the seemingly loosely defined label "Somocista," I wanted to learn how the Attorney General determined who was a Somocista. Most identified themselves by fleeing, I was told. Some of these were business partners of the Somoza family or officials of the National Guard or both. Others had obtained juicy loans from the public domain. The sticky cases were those where the owners had not fled but where neighboring campesinos and workers denounced an owner as a Somocista. The local prosecutor then had to conduct an investigation and proceed through the judicial system inherited from Somoza. Expropriated owners had a right to appeal their cases in the courts. As one government official commented to the *Miami Herald* about these land-owners, "They win some and they lose some."

Although it is not widely known, Nicaraguan law did not allow the confiscation of Somocista properties registered in the names of wives and dependents (provided they had not fled the country, of course). Given the barbarisms of the Somoza family, such respect for formalities was hard for me to comprehend. "We are trying to bring about justice within an inherited unjust legal framework—it's not easy," Ruth Herrera, a high-ranking Sandinista and General Secretary of the Ministry of Agricultural Development, told me.

Once all these cases had been decided, the government controlled 20 percent of Nicaragua's agricultural land, or about one-quarter of the large estates. That amounted to 43 percent of the total acreage in the large estates, those over 850 acres. Somoza himself had controlled about a third of the land that was confiscated, according to one rough (and unverified) estimate. The estates taken over by the government were for the most part large, modernized, export-oriented farms on the best soils and modern export-oriented cattle ranches. Two thirds of the land was made up of farms larger than 4,350 acres.

Obligation of Ownership

Although the large landowners supported the government takeover of Somocista lands, many watched anxiously for the government's *next* move. Wouldn't the new government—and all this talk of revolution—encourage peasant invasions of land on all capitalist farms and ranches? Wouldn't the new government set a ceiling on the amount of land any one person or family could own? Many landowners no doubt feared that private property was the real target of revolutionary change.

The Sandinistas, however, saw it differently. First, there were the practical considerations. The Sandinista leadership felt they couldn't take on any more land, even if they'd wanted to. The ministry was swamped by an enormous administrative undertaking once the government decided to organize state farms on the newly publicly owned land (see chapter seven). Many of the farms had been run down and abandoned by the Somocista owners who, in the final two years, had ceased to invest and sought only to liquidate their assets and get them to Miami. On some, land seizures and even military battles had taken their toll. On virtually all, production was at a standstill. Neighbors, relatives, and common thieves were smuggling abandoned machinery, irrigation equipment, and livestock off to Honduras and Costa Rica.

During my first visits I'd be bouncing along in a jeep with agricultural officials and every few minutes a message about some critical problem on one or the other of the 2,000 state farm units seemed to come across the CB system—"There's no truck"; "there's no seed"; "there's no payroll." Indeed, some agrarian reform officials feared they would become so tied up in day-to-day management problems of the state farms that it would be impossible to make further reforms. "Now we have to do the last thing any of us ever wanted to do—administer," Vice-Minister and Director General of the Agrarian Reform Salvador Mayorga told me with a look of frustration at the end of a typical sixteen-hour day two months into the revolution.

Second, the government resisted confiscating additional land because it was vitally concerned with reactivating production. It did not want to reduce production by taking land out of the hands of those using it efficiently. Nor did the government wish even to hint at land redistribution that might threaten landowners, giving them an excuse for not getting production going again.

Third, the Sandinistas' philosophy of agrarian reform is not anti-private property. Rather, the Sandinistas believe that the right to productive private property carries with it the obligation to use that property for the benefit of the society. Private property rights are guaranteed by the government but *only* if the owner is using the resource: owners letting their land lie idle, for example, will be subject to expropriation.

In actuality, however, the government did not take over additional land during the first two years, even if it were lying idle or being run down; the ministry had all the land it could handle. The only exceptions were farms where campesinos or farmworkers put tremendous pressure on the ministry.

More generally speaking, then, the goal of the Sandinistas has not been public ownership of all the means of production. It has sought public ownership primarily where it represents the only practical way to keep production going—as in the case of the farms abandoned by Somoza, or the national banking system, bankrupt as it was at the end of the war.

Indeed, two years into the revolution private ownership still prevailed. "Very few people realize that 80 percent of agricultural production is in the hands of the private sector, as is 75 percent of industrial production," a key official in the Ministry of Planning, Xabier Gorostiaga, pointed out at that time. The 20 percent of agricultural production that does belong to the state is deliberately called "Area of the People's

Property." "The Sandinistas want to instill in people the idea that this area belongs to the people. The state is not the owner, it is only the administrator," Gorostiaga commented.

A Further Obligation of Ownership

To the Sandinista leadership, the right to private property, as we have said, carries with it a positive obligation: to use that property for the benefit of the society. Its philosophy of private property also appears to carry with it a negative obligation: *not* to use that ownership as a basis for exploiting others or, stated another way, as a base for amassing wealth to the unfair advantage of others.

Therefore, while the government guaranteed the right to private property, in the first months of the revolution it established rent ceilings for agricultural land. The Sandinistas considered the prevailing rents to reflect the monopolization of land by a few that left the majority competing against each other for land. Moreover, they considered high rents, as well as sharecropping, to be disincentives to greater food production. The new rents work out to be about 85 percent less than the previous going rates. For corn and bean production, the maximum rent is now only about 100 córdobas ($10) per manzana (1.7 acres); for cotton, about three times as much.

Combined with government credit for small food producers, these rent controls would make a difference even in the first year for countless tenants, sharecroppers, and small producers, the Sandinistas hoped. One survey indicated that 10 percent of the laborers in the coffee harvest were able to cultivate corn and beans for the first time in their lives. Still, all did not go well: it now seems many landowners refused to rent at the legal rates. One apparently common landlord ploy was to refuse to lend oxen for plowing if the campesino insisted on the new rate. Only in those areas where the peasant and farmworker association, the ATC, was strong were the rent ceilings widely respected.

While many agrarian reforms have started by giving land titles to tenants and sharecroppers, the Sandinista agrarian reform appears much more conservative. In regard to rent, it no more interferes with private property than do urban rent control laws in many "free enterprise" industrial countries.

By making rents low and outlawing evictions, the Sandinistas sought to provide secure tenure to poor campesinos while side-stepping the bugbear of private property.

Socialize the Surplus

The fact that the new government sought to tie these obligations to the right to private property does not mean that it hoped the capitalist sector would be hamstrung and eventually wither away. The goal, according to Minister of Agricultural Development Jaime Wheelock, is not to socialize (bring under public control) all the means of production but instead to socialize (use for the public good) the surplus that the private sector produces. The government sought to allow the private producer a decent rate of profit but tap the additional surplus. This surplus could be tapped by mechanisms common in most capitalist societies, such as control over credit, export sales, foreign exchange, land use, labor relations, prices and marketing, and, of course, taxation. One of the first acts of the new government, consistent with this philosophy, was to establish the Ministry of Foreign Trade to handle the marketing of almost all exports, thereby putting an end to private producers falsifying foreign sales and depositing the proceeds in Miami or Panama bank accounts.

As we'll see in chapter five, the Sandinistas went to great lengths to try to foster the confidence of private producers and to keep them producing.

FIVE

THE FAILED PARTNERSHIP: BIG GROWERS AND THE STATE

WHEN MANY NORTH AMERICANS IMAGINE "revolutionary Nicaragua," they assume that all the land once belonging to the big plantation owners must now be in the hands of hungry peasants. Not so. Recall that only lands belonging to Somoza and his close associates were confiscated by the government after the fall of the dictatorship.

For the first three months after the victory, the new government thought it had control over 60 percent of Nicaragua's agricultural land. But at a planning session in late October 1979 in Jaime Wheelock's office, a young researcher presented us with startling new estimates which caused an anxious stir in the room. The large and medium-size farmers and ranchers, he reported, controlled over two-thirds of the agricultural land. They accounted for 72 percent of cotton production, 53 percent of coffee, 58 percent of cattle, and 51 percent of sugarcane. (See tables, pp. 100–110.)

Could private capitalist farmers and ranchers be counted on to maintain and expand urgently needed production? That became the big question for the rest of the afternoon session.

Without public control over the bulk of the export production, the new government realized that the recovery of the economy would hinge in large part on how effectively it could motivate these private growers to revive and eventually step up production. This partnership in the countryside was the heart of the new Nicaragua's plans for a "mixed economy."

Aware of their importance to the economy, the large and medium-size growers organized into producers' associations and drove some hard bargains. Not all the negotiations were formal. It was not unusual for government officials to spend Sunday afternoons in the countryside chatting with, say, some cotton growers to determine just what were their complaints and demands. Moreover, a number of leaders and other officials of the new government came from major land-owning families; they could readily test government proposals on close relatives and family friends.

While the government appealed to patriotic desires to rebuild a better Nicaragua, it was not overly idealistic or naive. In fact, the new government offered the private producers a package of incentives unprecedented even under the Somoza dictatorship:

—Enough credit, at an interest rate below the rate of inflation, to cover all working costs (seeds, fertilizers, fuel, equipment repair and replacement, all wages).

—Guaranteed prices for export crops, calculated to ensure a profit, and renegotiated yearly with the producers' associations in advance of annual planting. The government promised to absorb any drop in international commodity prices but to share with producers the benefits of any unexpected price rises.

—Low-cost government financing for replanting coffee trees infested by coffee blight.

—A seat for the association representing big growers and ranchers (UPANIC) on the Council of State and on various technical commissions.

—Rent decreases, primarily intended to help peasant producers, which also benefited many commercial growers, especially in cotton. In the mid-1970s, 40 percent of cotton growers rented their land from absentee owners, many residing in Miami and California.

—Low taxes on personal income and company profits.

Under this incentive package, the government put up the working capital, guaranteed minimum prices at which any reasonably efficient producer could make a profit, and absorbed any sudden drops in international market prices, while allowing the producers to own (as well as sell and bequeath) the land and equipment. It was tantamount to paying big producers a salary with bonuses tied to performance.

Why such a sweet deal? First, the government didn't want to drive the big producers out since it couldn't take on any more farms and ranches itself. Its hands were full dealing with the Somocista properties. Moreover, the government didn't want the big producers to leave the country because they constituted so much of the nation's scarce technical and administrative experience.

Behind the government overtures to the commercial producers were two other assumptions. The government believed that these incentives would stimulate production, especially of export crops. Through the foreign exchange earned, the government would gain funds it desperately needed for redistributive development as well as social programs. This would be especially true, the reasoning went, since the government had nationalized virtually all export trade and maintained a low rate of exchange, paying producers the official 10 córdobas per dollar, whereas the legal private ("parallel") market gave 25 to 40 córdobas to the dollar. In February 1982 this exchange rate was modified in favor of the producers as a further effort to stimulate production: producers could obtain part of the value of their exports effectively in dollars. Second, the Sandinistas believed that national unity was essential in the face of foreign hostility. By not nationalizing private producers and instead building their confidence in the new government, the Sandinistas hoped to avoid a confrontation that might give the U.S. government a rationalization for intervention in Nicaragua.

All this sounds reasonable. But did it work? In the judgment of many, it did not.

At a late night meeting on the eve of the second anniversary, a high official told me, "The private farmers, the big ones and the medium-size ones, have blown an historic opportunity. Once we might have thought we could rely on the private sector at least for a holding action. But now we see most of them are taking us backward economically." In his view, the majority of big producers not only failed to revive production but were systematically draining the rural economy.

Why Did They "Blow It"?

What looked to the Sandinistas like liberal offers may not have seemed so to the big growers, who believed they were losing a great deal. Under Somoza the big growers had unlimited access to cheap labor. Now with lowered land rents, increased employment on the state farms, and substantial government credit going to campesino producers, many poor peasants in the countryside saw themselves freed from the need to seek demeaning and arduous plantation work. "The *patrón* can't humiliate us anymore," is the way I have heard many of them put it. With fewer workers competing for jobs, for the first time the big growers had to negotiate with workers. And under the new order, not only was there no National Guard to prevent agricultural workers from organizing, but the government actually encouraged unions. To the Sandinistas, such worker organizations are the motor force of agrarian change.

"It's unbelievable," an old field hand told me, radiating with satisfaction. The ATC association on a cotton plantation near León had gotten the plantation owner to pay for the workers' medical treatments. Previously, the only medical bills the owner paid were for the horses. On another plantation, when the owner refused to pay the minimum wage, workers organized an ATC local. When the landowner attempted to break up the organization, the workers first struck; then they took over the plantation.

The big growers saw their profits threatened as the government sought to enforce the minimum wage law, mandated improvements in living and working conditions, and directly competed with the owners' price-gouging "company stores" by offering the rural poor basic goods at fixed low prices. Even though all these changes were not effective everywhere overnight, the direction was clear.

Despite these changes, the big growers knew that they could continue to make good profits. After talking with many of them, I'm convinced that their fears for the future were what caused them to dig in their heels against the new government. Knowing that the countryside was alive with the demands of hundreds of thousands of people who had been ruthlessly exploited for generations, it was *la Revolución* that threatened them. And perhaps it was inevitable that at the beginning of a revolution the fears of the rich affect their behavior so that their fears are self-fulfilling. Certainly, as we will see, that seems to be the case in Nicaragua.

Throughout the first year or so, the majority of private agricultural producers appeared undecided about how much they would cooperate with the new government. For one thing, since the Carter administration seemed willing to live with the new order in Managua, many of Nicaragua's agrarian capitalists felt incapable of effectively mobilizing themselves politically and economically against the new government. Still there was a palpable uneasiness and suspicion on every side, each feeding on the other's fears.

After the election of President Reagan, whose party platform called for the overthrow of the Nicaraguan government, the mood in the countryside was expectant. Adding to the tension was a serious incident in late November 1981 which revealed that at least some big growers had moved into direct sabotage of the new government and its agrarian program. Jorge Salazar, president of the Union of Nicaraguan Agricultural Producers (UPANIC), was discovered by police to be carrying concealed arms in his car and was killed in a shoot-out with police. Investigations revealed that Salazar and others, including the president of the Rice-Planters Association, planned to assassinate Sandinista leaders in coordination with an invasion by Somocista elements.

"Death by a Million Cuts"

Visiting Nicaragua at the end of 1980, I found Sandinistas and opponents alike predicting that 1981 would test the partnership between the big growers and the state. I returned to Nicaragua twice during the first half of 1981. I found the ATC, the newly created association of small and medium-sized farmers and ranchers (UNAG), the pro-Sandinista media, rural workers, and government officials themselves all accusing private producers of "decapitalization." Decapitalization referred to a range of economic sabotage by some large private farmers and ranchers:

—Cutting back on cultivated acres.

—Laying off needed workers and technicians.

—Selling off machinery and livestock, often to buyers in Honduras and Costa Rica.

—Using government production loans fraudulently—converting part of the loan to dollars on the street market, then sending the dollars to foreign bank accounts.

—Over-invoicing for imported machinery, spare parts, fertilizers, pesticides and so on in cooperation with "friendly" corporations in Guatemala or Florida. (The grower or rancher, arguing that the imported item is essential for production, gets dollars from the national bank—at the 10 to 1 rate rather than the 25 to 1 rate on the street market—plus, perhaps, a loan. The extra dollars wind up in a Miami bank account.)

—Faking or inflating fees and commissions to foreign firms or individuals, again as a way to siphon dollars out of the country.

—Paying excessive salaries, often in advance, to themselves and their family members.

—Asking for a government loan on the grounds of "saving jobs" once any combination of the above had caused financial losses.

The whole process adds up to "death by a million cuts," a top government economic planning advisor told me in June 1981. "It's not as if there are just four or five of the big guys," he explained. "If there were, you could round up one or two and make an example of them." Knowing that I was a *norteamericano*, he added, "It's like moonshine in Kentucky." There's one big difference though: in Nicaragua the "moonshining" undermines the entire economy.

In his opinion, the Sandinistas had originally underestimated the danger of decapitalization because they had underestimated the number and importance of the medium-size producers. By mid-1981, some ranches and farms were so decapitalized that, counting in debts, their value was negative. Specific examples of decapitalization have frequently been pointed out by campesinos and farmworkers and their organizations. Of the almost 900 acres of the Hacienda San Pedro in southeastern Nicaragua, approximately 100 grow coffee trees. In July 1981 the ATC charged that a large portion of the trees were ruined or on the verge of ruin because of lack of weeding and control of the coffee blight. The hacienda's 1980–81 coffee harvest dropped to one quarter what it had been the year before. The ATC claimed that by mid-1981, 70 percent of the capitalist farms and ranches in the region had been similarly neglected.

On his 2,800-acre Hacienda Namaslí, near the Honduran border, Alfonso Ramos had 800 acres in coffee trees. In 1980 he got credit from the National Development Bank to cover all projected production expenses. Yet it looked abandoned to a journalist visiting the hacienda in June 1981.

Before the revolution, Ramos employed 200 workers; in 1981, only 27. Left unattended, the coffee trees were hard hit by the coffee blight. When coffee trees are not cared for with weeding, fertilizer, pest control, yields are reduced for years to come. Ramos had also stripped the estate of almost all the machinery, including seven tractors, harvesters, and irrigation pumps—some taken into Honduras. An investigation revealed that he had sold the machinery, converted the money into dollars, and smuggled them out of the country.

Beef production also suffered from economic sabotage. By mid-1981, the government estimated that over 200,000 head of cattle had been rustled across the Honduran border since the start of the revolution. (Exports of beef from Honduras showed a sudden and inexplicable jump of 20 percent.)

In June 1981, the San Martín slaughterhouse laid off its 188 workers and announced it was closing for at least two months. The owners claimed a lack of animals, but the local ATC disputed this excuse. After borrowing money from the National Development Bank, the owners had sent checks totaling over $100,000 to Miami and had withdrawn seven million córdobas from the company accounts to buy dollars in the street, the government charged. The owners, all vociferous critics of the government, included the head of COSEP, the powerful big business chamber of commerce. Decapitalization hurt sugar production, too. The sugar mill on the San Pedro hacienda mentioned above used to grind 5,000 bundles of cane daily; in 1981 it did not grind any at all. In 1981, the Ministry of Agricultural Development charged that a large number of landowners simply refused either to cultivate or to rent out their lands. Some 30 percent of the normally cultivated land was being left idle, the ministry estimated in July. Driving through the Pacific Coast and Matagalpa and Estelí regions in June and July, I saw fields covered with weeds and pasture grass where the land had obviously been plowed and planted in previous years.

A Bad "Climate"?

A vicious circle of self-fulfilling prophecies was at work. The more landowners decapitalized, the more they were denounced by workers and by the government, and the more insecure all landowners felt (and were). Thus the circle starts again, but this time with more people.

Hitchhiking in Managua in June 1981, I was picked up by a coffee planter in a tinted-windowed Mercedes. He insisted on speaking English and kept calling me "friend." Earlier in the year he had come back to the country from Coconut Grove to "get out what I could while I could," he told me. He was frightened by the worsening "climate," by the mood of more and more workers and campesinos pressuring the government for a harder line (*mano dura*) toward the landowners. The threat of the worsening "climate"—fear of eventual expropriation—is the reason landowners most frequently give for decapitalization.

Yet even Somoza and the National Guard had not provided a secure climate for the wealthy. For years before the Sandinista-led victory over Somoza, those who could often sent their money out of the country. They feared that one day Somoza would fall, despite all the U.S. backing, and they would lose their capital. With the war, of course, the process accelerated. A United Nations commission estimated that $800 million was taken out of the country between 1977 and July 1979. In the last six months of the Somoza dynasty, $315 million disappeared from the country, equivalent to three quarters of the nation's total export earnings in a good year.

In the new Nicaragua, landowners have found themselves facing two options. One option is to make some córdobas by, say, growing cotton. This option means wading through government paperwork, hassling with increasingly demanding workers, locating spare parts, worrying about the weather and wondering if enough laborers can be hired for the harvest and at what price. The other option is to decapitalize, to sell off assets to get some córdobas which can be exchanged for dollars on the street market. With dollars one can either speculate on their value going up, deposit them outside the country, or go to Miami and buy clothing, appliances, and gadgets for resale in Nicaragua at a nice profit. Of course, an energetic landowner could do both: borrow, produce, and then use the profits to speculate in dollars, perhaps never paying back the government loan. Thus it's hardly an exaggeration when the government calls the big operators who are investing in long-term production "patriotic."

Decapitalization as a Political Weapon

Decapitalization could be understood as simply the big operators looking out for their individual interests. Their actions, however, take on political dimensions whether or not they are directly intended. Production failures that the big landowners themselves help to generate can later be cited as proof that the Sandinista-led government is a failure. Those who criticize the government most loudly for failure to meet production targets are often decapitalizing rather than producing, Sandinista Directorate member Bayardo Arce stated in March 1981.

At least some big landowners actually use decapitalization as deliberate provocation, many believe. If the big landowners can force the government to feel it must take over farms or businesses to keep the economy from collapse, these confiscations can then be cited as proof that the government is "repressive" and "communist." Such "proof" can weaken international support, making it harder for the government to get foreign financial aid. Moreover, some of the dollars drained out of the country by the big landowners probably finance the ex-National Guardsmen training in Florida and Honduras who are responsible for murderous raids on campesinos, teachers, and health workers in the northern border regions.

The Peasants React

Decapitalization of farms and ranches often outrages agricultural workers and campesinos. To them it is far from an abstract concept; they experience its consequences in "flesh and bones," as they say in Spanish. Poor workers, having responded to the government's pleas to restrain their own wage demands in the interests of the nation, then see the extreme selfishness of those infinitely better off than they. In visits to Nicaragua in the first half of 1981, I found widespread anger in the countryside against decapitalizers.

Angry workers on a cotton plantation near Chinandega told me that the *patrón* had taken out a $50,000 loan from the government to import a new tractor from the United States. They led me to a shed where they showed me a beat-up old Ford tractor that the *patrón* in fact bought locally for only a fraction of the loan, probably depositing the rest in a Miami bank account.

In late June 1981, a large group of campesinos from the interior of the country marched into Managua. "We have been forced to farm small plots of marginal land, trying to grow enough food," one of them told the press. "And now we see the gentlemen farmers letting hundreds and hundreds of acres of good land go idle."

The ATC made it clear that if owners were not disposed to plant, its members were. It was not an idle threat. In numerous cases the ATC moved in to complete the coffee harvest when private estate owners fired workers or left trees unpicked.

In the months leading up to the second anniversary, more and more campesinos and rural workers took it upon themselves to implement the government's dictum: no ownership without obligation. Land seizures increased. Often working with the ATC, the largest association of agricultural workers, and UNAG, the union of small producers, they took over the farms and ranches of those unwilling to fulfill the responsibility of ownership.

In June 1981 alone, the San Pedro hacienda, the Rio de Janeiro hacienda, the Namaslí farm, the San Martin slaughterhouse and numerous other properties were taken over by workers and campesinos. In Nueva Segovia, Jinotega and Matagalpa, hundreds of campesinos and workers seized decapitalized farms. The ATC and UNAG leaderships pressured the government to legalize what they considered just seizures—and to do so quickly. "Childrens' stomachs cannot wait," they argued.

The direct action of campesinos and landless farmworkers made it impossible for the public or the government to ignore the issue. Especially in the two months building up to the second anniversary celebrations, union meetings, press conferences, official speeches, and articles and editorials in the two pro-revolution newspapers all denounced decapitalization. On July 8, I watched a demonstration of workers and campesinos from many parts of the country in front of the Government House. They demanded that the government take measures against decapitalization; they suggested confiscation. "Contra la descapitalización—confiscación," the campesinos and workers chanted over and over.

The decapitalization law on the books since March 1980 was absurdly ineffective. The government had to prove in the courts that the owner had decapitalized before the state could intervene, and the courts were inadequate to move quickly. Moreover, the law required legal proof that assets or dollars had been taken out of the country—something rarely possible. The process took so long that by the time the courts decided against the owner, it was literally too late.

"Yes, against decapitalization, confiscation," declared Edgardo Garcia, head of the ATC, at a news conference. "But *timely* confiscation—not when there's nothing left but ruins, debts and a bankrupt farm." As a final absurd touch, the existing law also required the government to pay the owner the value of anything expropriated even if it got only an empty shell; this was tantamount to a financial incentive to decapitalize.

The campesinos and workers were demanding a law of

"preventive intervention." Under this law, the farmworkers' accusation that a landowner was selling off his machinery would be sufficient not only for an investigation but for an immediate confiscation of the farm by the Ministry of Agricultural Development. If the investigation proved the owner innocent of the charges, the property would be returned to him or her. Decapitalization should include taking money out of a production unit and not necessarily out of the country, the ATC demanded.

Implied in such a law would be a greater role for workers and campesinos. Already in May the ATC had organized 25 workshops to help farm workers detect and deal with decapitalization. The Sandinista newspaper *Barricada* commented, "In the private sector the workers are pressuring more and more to penetrate the 'secrets' of production." Workers now wanted the right to access to the financial information of the finca or ranch. "The financial data really belong to the people because, after all, they had to be given to the people's bank to get the loans for building production," a coffee estate worker commented. Edgardo Garcia, secretary general of the ATC, insisted that the National Development Bank should immediately respond when the farm's union asked for information about the bank's financing of the farm.

In the government's view, it had given the private sector an "historic opportunity" to enter into a mutually beneficial partnership. While many "patriotic producers" continued to develop their property, the government concluded that, for the most part, the big operators "blew it."

By the eve of the second anniversary in July 1981, workers, peasants, and big owners alike waited tensely to see how the government would change "the rules of the game."

SIX

SPILLING CREDIT IN THE COUNTRYSIDE

I MAGINE YOURSELF A PEASANT WITH SIX ACRES
of land on a Nicaraguan hillside, four days by mule from
the nearest town. One afternoon in early 1980, you suddenly
hear the thump-thump of a helicopter. A few minutes later
the helicopter lands fifty yards away and a young fellow steps
out saying he is from the Agrarian Reform ministry. He offers
you a loan to produce more corn and beans. The interest
rate? 11 percent—one third the rate of inflation. Is this a
dream? Is this the revolution?

Small farmers are among the poorest people in Nicaragua,
isolated on the poorest soils and on plots often too small
even to support their own families. Because their plots are so
small and their soil poor, two-thirds of them cannot survive
from their own direct production. They are forced to seek
supplemental wage work during other people's harvests.

While they use only 14 percent of the farmland, these
200,000 small farmers produce about 60 percent of Nicaragua's corn and beans, the basis of the national diet. "Small
farmers" refers to both owners and renters cultivating about
34 acres or less—much less in many cases. They represent 76
percent of the total number of farms.

Perhaps no segment of Nicaraguan society has experienced
such a dramatic economic change in the new Nicaragua.

Most small producers had never before received government credit, the kind of credit that even American farmers expect from their government. In the first year after the triumph, almost half the small farmers got government credit—and at low interest rates. Small producers got seven times more credit in 1980 than in the year before victory, 1978.

The Sandinistas had several motives for this massive small farm credit program. First, under Somoza the country increasingly had turned to imports to ensure enough of the national diet—corn and beans, the foods the small producers grow. Food production was neglected in favor of export production; then came the war's disruption. Now, if small producers would use the credit to buy the fertilizer, seeds and tools they need to significantly increase production, the country could save needed foreign exchange.

Second, "spilling credit on the countryside," as Jaime Wheelock called it, was, along with the literacy campaign, the best way the Sandinistas could think of to make the revolution real for the campesinos immediately. Having fought for years in the countryside, the Sandinistas had become intimately aware of the plight of small producers, whose only credit sources were landlords, moneylenders and merchants who charged usurious rates of interest. Thousands of small farmers had actively supported the Sandinistas during the war. So the Sandinistas wanted to express their gratitude as well as to build support for the difficult times ahead.

Third, the government wanted to help make up for the earnings lost to poor campesinos due to a steep drop in the number of harvest jobs because of war-related cutbacks in cotton acreage.

Finally, the Sandinistas viewed the credit program as an organizing tool. With the enticement of lower interest rates for cooperatives than for individuals (8 percent compared to 11 percent), the government hoped to encourage small producers to form cooperatives or credit associations. From the administrative viewpoint, working with cooperatives was much easier than dealing with thousands of individuals. Sandinistas also tended to see cooperatives, however rudimentary, as facilitating social advancement (literacy, modernization of production, culture, public health) compared to isolated, individual production.

"...the generosity of revolutionaries."

While the leaders' logic and good intentions in distributing credit massively in 1980 seemed impeccable, not everything turned out quite as hoped. Looking back on the experience a year and a half later, Jaime Wheelock commented, "These are mistakes made out of a romanticism which, in a sense, is a negative result of the generosity of revolutionaries."

First was the sheer administrative challenge to a ministry that itself was less than one year old. Because of the logistical difficulties of getting credit to tens of thousands of farmers often in remote areas, some campesinos received credit so late that they were still harvesting their corn and beans when the season arrived when their labor was desperately needed on the export crop farms.

Second, crop yields in at least several regions were lower than ministry projections. The problem was compounded by the fact that the government had set a low guaranteed purchasing price for corn and beans, based on its somewhat optimistic calculations of producer costs. Thus some small producers simply didn't earn enough for their crop to repay the loans, although they were free to sell to private buyers at higher prices than the government guaranteed.

Third, in incredibly inaccessible areas (remember the helicopter!) farmers received credit, but then no one came to buy their harvests. According to the ministry, up to 50,000 acres of corn and beans (about 10 percent of the crops) may have been "lost" in this fashion. Realizing they had no one to buy what they had produced, some campesinos harvested only what they could use for themselves and their animals. (This did allow them to eat better than before.)

Finally, the credit that many received simply exceeded the economic potential of their land. So even if a campesino family could get all the seeds, fertilizers, tools and work animals they could use, the money obtained from selling their crops was nowhere near enough to pay back the credit. Because campesino families probably consumed more than ever before, indebtedness was made even more likely. Thus, even with good crops, many did not sell enough (or get a high enough price) to avoid winding up in debt.

So despite all the good intentions, studies of the 1980

"spilling of credit" to campesinos showed that the increased credit had little impact on production, in part because much of the credit was used for consumption—a new pair of shoes, sugar, kerosene—rather than production.

Indebtedness Crisis

Compounding this disappointment, the repayment rates on the loans turned out to be less than hoped for. As in most countries, however, small producers performed better than larger producers (or state farms) in repaying their debts. Before long, a growing number of small producers were demanding that their debts be forgiven. Moreover, the minority of small producers who had received loans from the Somoza banks (now nationalized) wanted them wiped out. But many government policymakers feared that debt forgiveness would set a bad and difficult-to-reverse precedent. And bank officials worried over the government's growing fiscal crisis. Foreign loans to finance more credit would burden the economy for decades to come.

With the bad record of repayments the first year, national bank officials were reluctant to renew lending to small producers for 1981. But the ATC and the Ministry of Agricultural Development, with its influential director Jaime Wheelock, pressed. With the government-wide decision in March 1981 to launch an all-out food production push, the balance of power settled in favor of renewing credit for small producers, although the total amount was significantly reduced.

The long debate, unfortunately, delayed the distribution of new credit. Delays in credit caused delays in planting in some areas. Around León, for example, only 25 of 68 small farmer cooperatives received timely credit, partially undermining the launching of the campaign to increase food production by small farmers.

The indebtedness problems of the first year reverberated in the second. Many campesinos who had been unable to repay the first loan refused loans the second and third time around. They feared that, as under the Somoza dictatorship, the credit was offered only to set them up for foreclosure and seizure of the little land, animals and equipment they had.

"Today there are still poor campesinos who have the idea

that the government is going to trick them or rob them of their property," a campesino explained. "There are still campesinos who won't go to the bank because they are afraid they'll never see their money again."

For this reason, many campesinos applied for financing for only part of their land, keeping a "fallback area" in case of crop failure. In some regions where anti-government forces were particularly strong, this fear was exacerbated by anti-government commercial producers and others. They told the campesinos that the government's generous offering of loans was a "communist" trick to take their land—and even their children—away from them.

Unplanned Beneficiaries

The Sandinistas wanted the poorest campesinos to be the prime beneficiaries of the new credit. But their hopes were frustrated by the failure of credit policies to explicitly and effectively favor the poor and by the unanticipated impact of inflation.

The rush of credit to so many small producers without corresponding increases in the availability of farm inputs set off a sudden price spiral in the countryside for work animals, tools, seeds, fertilizers, pesticides and transportation. Because many campesinos used the unprecedented cash which the loans put in their pockets to satisfy pent-up desires for sugar, salt, shoes, clothing and other consumer goods, their prices jumped too.

Inflation, as always, hit the poorer campesinos harder. The real beneficiaries turned out to be the rural middle class—truck owners, merchants and the richer campesinos with animals and equipment to rent. They gained in profits and assets as the flood of credit intended primarily for poor campesino producers rebounded to them.

Moreover, even though the majority of the campesinos receiving bank credit for the first time were probably the poor, most of the total *amount* of small-producer credit did not go to them. There were no special lower interest rates for the most disadvantaged campesinos. Nor did they get more favorable prices when buying inputs or transporting their crops.

Thus the outcome of Nicaragua's rural credit program

turned out not very different from those in other countries around the world. In our investigations at the Institute for Food and Development Policy we have seen, again and again, how the better-off small producers corner the benefits of most small-producer credit programs. The better-off small producers—the minority who generally work their land mostly with hired labor—have all the advantages. They own their farms, have registered titles, and thus can offer the bank collateral. They are experienced in working with the government and have developed better entrepreneurial skills. Not surprisingly, therefore, most of the multiple-year credit went to them, credit they could use to buy young animals to fatten or to put in coffee or fruit trees.

Landholders too large to qualify for the subsidized small producer interest rate actually received considerable credit, subsequent ministry investigations discovered. In the *departmento* of Boaco, statistics on this type of lending were deliberately kept off the records, while bank officers in two other regions only considered for credit those with nine acres or more, even though the majority had less. (*Poder Sandinista*, a Sandinista Front supplèment to *Barricada*, denounced the practice.)

In one region with unusually good data, the rich campesinos, who are small coffee producers, got six times more credit per family than the poor campesinos, who are tenants producing corn and beans. This provoked fears within the new government that small coffee farmers could become an elite among small farmers, dampening enthusiasm for the food production so urgently needed. Tenants with experience in planting got twice as much credit as farmworkers getting access to land for the first time.

For all these problems and injustices, however, we should not forget that even in the first year over 70,000 campesino families obtained bank credit for the first time in their lives. *Relatively speaking*, they experienced the most dramatic change of all producers.

Lessons

While many people might assume that policies aimed at justice should treat all farmers the same, Nicaragua's leaders have learned it's more complicated than that. To be effective in favoring the poorest, they have learned, it takes time, organization, and mobilization to identify the different social strata within the peasantry, much less design and implement unequal policies for unequal people. (This task is especially unlikely and difficult during a food production emergency.)

To many North Americans it might seem quite reasonable that the better-off campesinos get the lion's share of the credit; after all, they have the most land and animals to work with and the most experience. But what appears "reasonable" might not be if the goal is not only to produce more food but to ensure that more underfed people are able to eat from their own production. To achieve this goal it is necessary to take a course which might at first appear slower and therefore less efficient. Yet favoring the poorer, less secure, less experienced producers might turn out to be the best course to eradicate hunger.

Finally, even at its worst, the new government's track record in credit for small farmers is a far cry from the small farmer credit programs financed by the U.S. Agency for International Development under Somoza. In these programs an estimated 80 percent of the total credit went right off the top to the big export operators.

What has impressed us is that the new government recognized and publicly acknowledged the unintended consequences of its credit policies. This is in stark contrast to so many governments and international lending agencies, such as the World Bank, which often try to cover up the fact that the well-off benefit disproportionately from their rural assistance programs, often to the detriment of the true poor.

SEVEN

THE STATE FARM: DISCREDITED MODEL OR PRAGMATIC ADAPTATION?

"UP THE STEPS, THROUGH THE FRENCH doors and into what was once the living room. The Miami-chic 'still life' in gilded frame still hangs on the wall; a large fringed hammock with 'SOMOZA' woven on the side is slung across a corner. A set of shelves bear model ships, crystal ornaments, china horses and six mugs with naked-lady handles, posing provocatively over the rims.

"Under this display sits a labourer on a sofa with muddy boots and work clothes, a booklet *The Role of Unions in the Revolution* in his cowboy hands. Another is looking at the cartoon version of the Economic Plan for 1980. Together with the four others in the room, all leaders of the local ATC, they have a study session, held every week. This is the first time that the meeting has been held in the former land-owner's house; old taboos die hard. Outside, other farm la-bourers and their children cavort in the swimming pool. The people have finally reappropriated their property."

This description of a ranch near Boaco which had be-longed to Somoza's uncle comes from the diary of Hermione Harris, a British development worker who lived in Nicaragua for several years. The ranch was a state enterprise at the time she visited, a few months after victory.

To many North Americans, "state farms" evoke the worst

of socialist dogmatism and bureaucratic incompetence. Some might agree with the standard ideological justification that on state farms "the people" own the land (via the government) so that the whole society supposedly benefits. They might also agree that because the farms are controlled by the state, rational agricultural planning becomes possible for the first time. But, most North Americans would ask, haven't state farms proven themselves production fiascos in the Soviet Union and Eastern Europe? Don't the workers come to feel as alienated as on any private estate? Doesn't state planning lead to inflexible directives out of touch with local realities? With such doubts in mind, most North Americans, upon hearing about state farms in Nicaragua, assume that revolutionary leaders are once more clinging to a discredited model.

Nonetheless, the Sandinista leadership is adamant in denying that their decision to convert confiscated Somocista etates into state farms was a "knee jerk" socialist response. They reject any suggestion that they were opting to follow a Soviet (or Cuban) blazed path. Rather they felt they had no option. "We were not choosing a model," commented Jaime Wheelock. "The model was chosen for us by the realities."

First, the Sandinistas feared that if the 2,000 or so confiscated properties were parcelled up, productivity would drop. Two months after the final victory, Luis Franco, a Christian Brother appointed to coordinate government services to cooperatives in the province of León, explained to Oxfam America's Michael Scott:

"The production units formerly owned by the Somozas, the military and their associates were large, highly mechanized plantations into which huge investments in the millions were channeled, often from the national treasury. Breaking them up into a myriad of parcels would decrease or eliminate the possibility of employing the technology and machinery that had been put into them and, consequently, would reduce their productivity. We realized that it was absolutely necessary to keep the production units intact. Had we not [acted] immediately, the campesinos would have occupied this land themselves and would have parceled it out in the traditional way." Indeed, I was told that the Sandinistas had

to act swiftly after triumph to minimize sacking of the Somocista farms by workers and campesinos in several areas of the
country.

A second rationale for state farms is that parcelling out the
land would inevitably be unjust. How would it be decided
who should get a parcel? Only permanent workers on the
farm? What about seasonal workers who are often worse off?
Jaime Wheelock, like Solomon, shunned such a decision:
"Distributing the land is easier said than done. . . . What do
you do in the case of a sugar cane plantation where there's
only one processing plant? Who gets that? How do you decide who should get the choice parcels?"

Third, the Sandinistas thought it would be easier to create
more jobs—so desperately needed by landless farmworkers—
on large farms than on small parcels worked by family labor.

One way to keep the confiscated farms intact would have
been to continue and extend the previctory *comunas*. *Comunas* were cooperatively worked farms that campesinos and
farmworkers in some liberated areas hurriedly set up after
they seized Somocista lands. Yet soon after triumph the Sandinistas concluded that for the sake of production they had
to ask the peasants to hand this land over to the state. It was
a difficult decision: "Is there any precedent for undoing after
victory the agrarian reform model that was carried out during
the insurrection?" agrarian reform director Salvador Mayorga asked me during my first visit. That the Sandinistas succeeded in changing the war-time *comunas* into state farms
without much conflict testifies to the moral authority of
the Sandinistas in the eyes of the campesinos and landless
workers.

But why did the Sandinistas opt for state farms over
comunas?

Painfully aware of the financial and production crisis in
which the war left the country, the leadership of the agrarian
reform felt it had to do what would most quickly revive production. The *comunas* were actually functioning on only a
few farms. Organizing genuine cooperatives on the 2,000 or
so confiscated farms all over the country would take too
much time, they thought.

But the leadership perceived an even more basic problem

with encouraging more *comunas* on the confiscated land. With victory, restoring the nation's capacity to earn foreign exchange for a whole range of imports became just as much an emergency as producing food. And it was feared that if campesinos and farmworkers were granted direct control of the farms, almost all set up to produce for export, they would plant food crops instead. As state farms, the Sandinistas figured, the Somocista properties could continue to use their infrastructure to produce mostly for export, with profits going for the public's well-being. The Sandinistas were equally concerned about increasing food production, but they saw government support, especially credit, for the small campesino producers as the best way to achieve this goal. Land scarcity, they believed, was not the root of Nicaragua's food problem.

While Wheelock and other leaders stressed how circumstances dictated developing state farms on the confiscated land, the Sandinistas nonetheless expected some positive consequences. They hoped, for example, that state farms would foster worker participation in management and that, more than with individual farms or cooperatives, the profits could be used to benefit the poor majority in Nicaragua. Also, the Sandinistas believed they could avoid some of the problems state farms have encountered elsewhere. Whereas state farms in the Soviet Union, for example, entailed the collectivization of small, privately owned farms, in Nicaragua the process involved simply the transfer to public ownership of already existing large, centrally managed farms.

For the first year and a half, just bringing some coherent organization into the over 2,000 confiscated farms was a major part of the work. Two or three neighboring farms were consolidated into State Production Units (U.P.E.'s), each with an administrator. These 800-odd U.P.E.'s in turn were grouped according to proximity and type of production into 170 *complejos* (complexes). Each *complejo* is under an administrator who appoints the U.P.E. administrators. Several *complejos* are organized into *empresas* (enterprises) that have a roughly similar production. Whereas in Nicaragua everyone refers to "U.P.E.'s," we will use the term "state farm." Bear in mind, however, that most "state farms" (U.P.E.'s) are a grouping of what once were several farms or ranches.

The Sandinistas' goal "is not to repeat the mistakes of the type of bureaucratic socialism that people have known up to now," according to Peter Marchetti, an American Jesuit priest who is a resident adviser on the agrarian reform. "Their principal goal is to continually, as much as they can, reduce the responsibility of bureaucratic units." He notes that in regard to state farms "the government has taken a very creative step and put each enterprise on its own with respect to the national bank. . . . Each unit [is] independent and has to work out its own efficiency."

Are State Farms Profitable?

Are the state farms generating an economic surplus? Or are they a net drain on the economy? Two years into the revolution, these questions were being debated at the highest levels of the government.

Most Americans, thinking of the U.S. Postal Service or Amtrak, probably expect the worst of state farms. They expect "lemon socialism," in which the public takes ownership of the inevitable money-losers in the economy while private corporations hang on to the lucrative operations. In June 1981, Augusto Zeledón, administrator of the ex-Somoza coffee farm La Fundadora, told me that every group of visiting foreigners asked him about the profits of the farm. "You can count on the question," he said. In fact, only an hour before, a U.S. visitor had asked him, "How are the profits divided?" He told her, "Well, we haven't had any yet to divide."

In examining the profitability of state farms it is easy to forget the past—how Somocista operations made their sizeable profits. They made such profits largely by exploiting workers—by paying less than even the minimum wage, by providing miserable working conditions, by laying off most workers for several months each year and by corruption. They helped drain the national treasury by fraudulent borrowing, making profits by building up debt. The state farms are also facing the same fiscal crisis devastating other export-oriented farms in Central America: higher prices for imported inputs such as fertilizer and pesticides and lower prices for the commodities produced.

Improved Services

During the first year or so, part of the farms' earnings were returned to the workers not only in the form of wages, but also in social services. Most of these services—clinics, schools, etc.—were built right on the farm. To avoid growing inequalities in standards of living between state farms, the government decided to organize these services, especially in health and education, on a *regional* level and through the Ministries of Health, Education, etc. A cattle ranch might invariably have a greater profit margin than, say, even an efficiently operated coffee plantation, given the relative value of beef and coffee—but should the ranch workers automatically benefit from better clinics or schools? In addition, the government wants to avoid concentrating social services on the minority of the rural population permanently employed on the state farms. Regionally organized services can also benefit seasonal laborers and campesinos and their families living in the region. "This is most important," note two scholars of Latin American agrarian history, "since other Latin American agrarian reforms, such as the Peruvian, have tended to exacerbate rural inequality by concentrating the provisions of social services in only the reformed sector, thus excluding the majority of the rural population."

Rather than each farm or grouping of farms using part of its earnings for social services, each will have to calculate its profits and, like a private firm, pay various taxes to the state. Each grouping of state farms also allocates money for investments on these farms. Some may be for better cultivation practices, such as mulch fertilization of coffee trees. In the short run these may mean higher costs and, therefore, lower profits, but they should provide greater productivity in the long run. Other investments, such as irrigation, intensify production and provide more year-round employment.

Profitability

It is hardly surprising that the state farm sector, for the most part, has been a drain on the government given these longer term investments, the problem of building new worker incentives, and the run-down condition in which many of the farms were taken over. In 1980, the state farms got over 25 percent of the total agricultural credit, yet produced only 14 percent of the value of agricultural production. In terms of loan repayment, an officer in the national finance corporation told me that the state is "our worst client."

At the same time, there has been considerable debate within the ministry about the notion of "profitability." Some have pointed out that the performance of the state farms cannot be measured in the same terms as private farms. For instance, the state farm policy of providing more year-round jobs may, at least in the short term, work against profitability. Some argue that the *volume* of production should be considered more important than profits (defined as revenue minus expenses). For it is the cotton, sugar or coffee (or locally grown food substituted for imported food) that earns the *dollars* or other "hard" currency that the economy needs. In this view of profitability, the only cost that truly makes a difference is the foreign exchange cost of *imported* inputs such as tractors and fertilizers. Proponents point out that córdoba costs are not the same for the state enterprise as for the private enterprise since the government can print córdobas, while private farms get them only in exchange for the the exports they sell through the government. They do caution that too many córdobas in circulation can be inflationary. Yet boosting the volume of exports, no matter what the córdoba cost, is the goal for them.

In its simplistic form, this approach could cover up gross inefficiency and lead to a flagrant disregard for cost accountability. Underlying this view on profitability, however, is the intriguing idea that, despite the increased expenditures for cash and social wages, the state agroexport enterprises would easily show a profit if the dollar-córdoba rate were revised from 10 to 1 to, say, 17 to 1 (bearing in mind that on the legal "parallel" or "tourist" market, the dollar easily fetches 25 to 1).

In 1981 the ministry decided to clear the state farms' books of pre-victory debts, at least those in dollars. Being saddled with enormous past debts, it was thought, would lead farm administrators and workers to despair of ever turning a profit, a despair that would become a self-fulfilling prophecy. Clearing the books has been difficult since Somoza and his associates often kept false records and had many bank records destroyed when the end seemed near.

Generally, costs in the state farm sector are running higher than expected—due, no doubt, to reduced labor productivity and administrative problems. If the trend is not reversed, it could easily jeopardize the state's ability to deliver on social services. (The early 1981 cutbacks in previously budgeted expenditures for "nonproductive" social service are an ominous warning.)

Measures are being taken to reverse the trend. First, as we have already stressed, a major effort is under way to develop accounting systems on the farm and *empresa* level. While some sort of bookkeeping was to be in place by mid-1981 on every farm, the target date for the full system is 1983.

The goal is to get a grip on whether a particular state farm is losing money or not. If it is, government thinking is that either changes must be made or a *deliberate* subsidy set. It is crucial to calculate and budget a precise and appropriate subsidy rather than say, "Oh, we don't run the dairy farm to make a profit anyway," an attitude that could easily cloak a multitude of needless inefficiencies.

Questions of profitability have helped lead to some key decisions regarding state farms which show how free the Sandinistas are from any Marxian dogmatism that state farms are inherently the "superior form of production." As we will see in a later chapter, after initial resistance, the government gave in to the demands of landless seasonal workers and campesinos for land to plant food crops by lending them idle lands on the state farms. Even more significant was a decision that state farms which cannot be operated profitably, because they are too small or too remote, or for any other reasons, would be turned over to independent cooperatives of landless campesinos. The government is also open to turning unprofitable state farms over to individual peasant families when the families are clearly not interested in cooperatives. By the end of July 1982, over 300 state farms had been titled over to peasants and landless laborers, comprising 40 percent of the land titled over in the first year of the Agrarian Reform Law.

Handing over lands in the state farm sector to land-hungry rural people reduces the pressure to expropriate idle or un-derutilized land on the private estates. For a government still trying to work out a productive *modus vivendi* with private commercial farmers, this has no doubt been an important consideration.

The leadership's state farm policy has responded to Nicaragua's historical circumstances and has resisted any idealized concept of either urban-based planners or ideologues. In chapter eleven we'll see that it has a similar policy on agricultural cooperatives. But first let's look into the difficult problems the state farms are tackling in trying to increase production while meeting the just demands of the workers.

EIGHT

WAGE AND PRODUCTIVITY DILEMMAS

"LET'S SUPPOSE THAT EACH OF YOU EARNS 1,000 córdobas a month, and we decide to double that to 2,000. What would happen? There would be more money on the street. Isn't that so? So the goods we have would be bought up very quickly, with more money around, and we would start to have shortages. And when shortages start, things begin to get more expensive. So that within a short time your 2,000 córdobas would buy the same that 1,000 córdobas bought you before."

Comandante Tomás Borge, the only surviving founder of the Sandinista Front, was talking to workers at the Pedro Rivas Recalde state farm. They were demanding higher wages to help offset the inflation which had already eaten up most of the increase in the minimum wage established soon after victory. Without more goods, Borge told them, more money is no help.

It was a message few workers wanted to hear. After the seemingly impossible victory over Somoza, anything seemed possible. Low wages had been one of the starkest signs of their oppression. So it was hard to understand why, with the dictatorship overthrown, they the workers couldn't immediately enjoy the profits once hoarded by the rich.

Under Somoza, labor legislation included a $2.10-a-*day* minimum wage for agricultural workers. But few workers ever got it. In practice, wages typically ranged from $.80 to $1.70 a day, except for skilled workers such as tractor operators. Mandatory fringe benefits, such as meals or transportation, were seldom delivered. Some workers have told me that they didn't even know such laws had ever been on the books. At the very best, it seems, Somoza sometimes enforced the rules when he wanted to teach particular growers a lesson.

A few months following victory the new government boosted the minimum wage by 30 percent. But because the government paid the minimum wage on state farms and attempted to enforce it elsewhere, the *average* rural wage may have gone up over 60 percent. Fringe benefits or equivalent cash payments amounted to further increases. (Well into the first year, however, administrators of some state farms paid less than the minimum wage, according to the Sandinista Front's newspaper *Barricada*. The explanation I was given in the Ministry was that some farms were *de facto* self-financing for many months, and the administrators did not have the money.)

Yet two years' inflation seemed to have cancelled out real gains in cash income for most permanent and seasonal workers on the state farms. During the insurrection, inflation was 80 percent annually. Since victory, it's been 25 to 35 percent a year with every indication that it will be rising over the foreseeable future. On the first anniversary the government raised the minimum agricultural wage 18 percent to help offset inflation. While some ministry people can calculate a few points' gain here or there (largely by costing in the fringe benefits), everyone admits that workers universally feel they are earning "*lo mismo*"—the same.

On many farms, state and private alike, workers have persisted in demanding higher wages. On some state farms workers have gone on strike. At the Altamira rice farm (formerly Somoza's, therefore now a state farm), workers struck for five days during March 1980. Strikes in early 1980 over wages at the sugar mills, the state-owned Ingenio Monterrosa and the huge, privately owned San Antonio, were particularly costly. Cut cane quickly rots and work stoppages at San Antonio were estimated to cost over one-half million córdobas ($50,000) a day.

The workers' ignorance of the cost accounting on each state enterprise exacerbated the conflict over cash wages. On a state-owned dairy farm in Managua, for instance, the unit production costs in 1980 were over 35 percent higher than the selling price. But the workers weren't told this. So, knowing that total production was up, they couldn't understand why their wages weren't also hiked. They were bewildered when told that the dairy farm was losing money.

In resisting wage demands, the Sandinista leadership has had to fend off opponents on both the left and right. Groups such as the Frente Obrero ("Workers Front," an ultraleft communist labor group) tell the workers that the Sandinistas, in their unwillingness to increase wages, are defending the country's monied interests. At the same time, the right-wing *La Prensa* tries to discredit the government by harping on the fact that workers' wages buy no more than before.

Government and Sandinista Front spokespeople invariably respond to wage demands by admitting that they are just, but saying they cannot be satisfied given the economic crisis of the nation. Leaders such as Jaime Wheelock have often gone personally to talk with disgruntled workers to explain the government's dilemma. When the Frente Obrero organized strikes at sugar mills calling for a 100 percent wage increase, the Sandinista Front's Organizing Secretary responded: "This miniscule organization [the Frente Obrero] is quite ignorant of the situation of the country and real problems that we face. They are making a series of proposals which are totally pie in the sky. These proposals are very nice, very interesting, but quite unrealizable."

The ATC has generally been successful in countering such groups. This success is the fruit of a long relationship of trust with the workers built by ATC leaders over years of organizing—under great risk—in many of the country's sugar mills and other agro-industrial centers. At the same time, the ATC has pushed for more health and housing improvements and for government stores selling basic foods at low fixed prices in the countryside.

Social Wage

In a similar vein, the government's primary response to the dilemma has been to try to shift the focus of rural workers' demands away from the cash wage to the "social wage," meaning improvements in health services, meals, housing, etc. Not only are they less inflationary than cash wage increases but they respond to the dire need (especially following the war) for improved living and working conditions. Many Sandinistas also favor increases in the "social wage" because they do not foster the individualism they feel would thwart the future development of the country.

The government has also responded to wage demands by trying to keep food prices down (so low wages could buy more) by importing an unprecedented quantity of staple foods during the first two years after the war. By 1981, the government set low fixed prices for the basic necessities (corn, beans, cooking oil, sugar, kerosene, soap, salt, etc.), and subsidized farmers.

In addition, the ministry set up ENABAS stores on 149 state farms serving over 16,000 families, or 8 percent of the rural population. The stores are managed by workers selected by the farms' labor unions. Unfortunately, these stores are not always as well stocked as hoped.

In retrospect one might judge that the *first* move of the new government in 1979 should have been to announce an economic emergency—austerity for all. Yet I know from conversations with Jaime Wheelock and other Sandinista leaders how repugnant it was to them to call for belt-tightening by the poor just after a war in which the poor paid the heaviest price. How difficult indeed when the poor can see all around them an elite loathe to sacrifice even imported luxuries, yet making political hay out of shortages and price increases.

Year-Round Work

The Sandinistas based their initial rural policies on the assumption that what many rural poor want, above all, is year-round work. Under Somoza, over a third of those working in agriculture were not only deprived of land but were employed only three or four months each year. So within one year after victory, the Sandinistas had doubled—even tripled—permanent employment on many state-run farms compared to when the same farms belonged to Somoza and his associates. With the rush of expectations after the overthrow of the dictatorship, every worker on a confiscated farm seemed to be badgering the administrators for a permanent job for a brother-in-law or a cousin or a friend who previously could get only seasonal work. Benjamin Linarte, administrator of the large Altamira rice complex, told me that if he took down the "no job openings" sign at the entrance, at least 150 people would show up looking for work on the first day alone. Many administrators obviously gave in. After all, the farm was the people's property, wasn't it? And surely these were "the people."

Many thus gained permanent work during the chaotic early period in which often there were no payrolls and the new books, for what they were worth, were kept at ministry headquarters in Managua. (It was two years after victory before the ministry knew the exact total of permanent workers on the state farms.)

The problem is, of course, that unless production increases at least as fast as the payroll grows, labor productivity (output per person-hour worked) plummets. That means it costs more to produce a pound of rice, sugar, or coffee. The Sandinistas have no short-term answer to the problem. In the short run, the ministry has attempted to use the additional workers for socially useful ends. On some farms, for instance, they build new on-farm services such as clinics and stores. On the Germán Pomares sugar complex, where all 1,015 workers are now permanently employed, many repair houses, buildings and roads during the "dead season." (About 400 of these workers had only seasonal work on the plantation "before.")

One obvious alternative would be to replace machines with hand work. Concerned about the many unemployed in his region, the administrator of the highly mechanized Altamira rice farm considered just such a move. He had many reservations, including the workers' fear that standing in irrigated fields would give them arthritis. But on my last visit to Altamira in March 1981 I saw so many giant John Deere tractors paralyzed for lack of spare parts that I wondered if he would not be forced to overcome his reservations.

In the longer term, the government hopes to be able to invest in irrigation so that food crops can be grown and harvested during the months before planting the export crop. Then there would be no "dead season." But given the falling and very low prices for Nicaragua's major exports, that day could be a long way off. The increasing difficulty of securing long-term loans from World Bank-type sources, largely because of opposition from the Reagan administration, would also make this more difficult. A more immediate measure to deal with the dead season is lending or renting unused land on state farms to workers who form production cooperatives, as we discuss in chapter eleven.

Falling Productivity

During the 1980 agricultural cycle, the state farms employed more persons per unit of land yet produced less value than the private capitalist farms. This falling productivity could not all be attributed to the additional number of workers given year-round employment. Perhaps even more significant was the fact that on many publicly owned farms, the average work day in practice has dropped from seven to about five hours or even less. When workers were paid to do a set piece of work, they finished as soon as possible, with quality often suffering.

Even the official work day, at least on some farms, has been reduced from eight to seven hours. On the state farm "La Sorpresa" in the province of Jinotega, a mid-1980 report stated that the work day had been reduced from eight to seven hours but that many workers put in only three. Field workers were completing only half as much work in a given day as compared to before the revolution. At the same time, the state-owned Germán Pomares sugar mill estimated that labor productivity had dropped at least 25 percent.

On the Altamira rice farm, the pilots of the small planes that sow the rice could optimally cover 182 acres an hour but were sowing scarcely 106 acres. When the pilots had been paid by the number of acres sown, they earned an average of 30,000 córdobas a month. Under the new order, they have a fixed monthly salary of 9,500 córdobas, only 500 córdobas less than the Minister of Agricultural Development earns. Why the falling productivity? From the outside one might be baffled. After all, wouldn't workers want to work *harder* now, hoping their production would benefit the whole country's development. In a December 1979 address to the national assembly of the ATC, Jaime Wheelock asked if workers on state farms were wage laborers? No, he answered, "they are producers of social wealth, and the consciousness of the producer is quite different from that of the wage laborer. . . . He knows that each stroke of the machete is no longer to create profits for a boss, but perhaps to create a new pair of shoes for a barefoot child who may be his own."

But agricultural laborers saw it differently, at least initially. They had labored at hard, tedious and even dangerous work for years to make others rich. The new order gave them an immediate chance for only one tangible good—less work. Many office-bound people in the ministry caricatured this notion as "Revolución es piñata," referring to the candy-filled paper animal batted about at parties. But many workers saw themselves taking what they called their "historic vacations." The fact that they can do so speaks to perhaps the most fundamental change in the new Nicaragua—the loss of fear. Workers don't feel in danger of being brutalized or fired by their employers.

Ruptured is the old system in which export crops were produced through repression (the National Guard, dismissal without just cause, unions effectively prohibited) and through depriving people of enough land (and credit and good prices) to provide any alternative means of survival. For decades the shortage of workers during peak harvest periods should have given workers bargaining power to win higher pay and better working conditions. But actual repression or very substantial threat of repression by the National Guard thwarted that natural development.

Many permanent agricultural laborers with a little parcel of land in food crops expanded it or rented land for the first time. Moreover, lowered rents and abundant credit led small farmers to reduce the time they put in on the "gran producción" in order to tend to their own crops. Workers staying home to work their own plots was the main cause of absenteeism on the Germán Pomares sugar complex, for example.

Wage Policy

The departure of technically trained managers for jobs on the private farms also probably contributed to the drop-off in labor productivity. A primary reason has been the difference in paychecks. As a matter of general policy, the new government has collapsed the differential between the highest- and lowest-paid public sector employees. The Minister of Agricultural Development, for instance, was paid only eight times as much as the lowest-paid permanent farm worker; the ratio had been 78 to 1 under Somoza. By reducing the higher salaries and raising the lower ones, salaries for state farm managers have averaged only somewhat over twice that of permanent workers or 2,611 córdobas ($261) a month, making it easier for private farms to lure away state farm managers with higher salaries.

My visits to state farms indicate that women generally receive lower wages than men. The administrator on the ex-Somoza coffee farm La Fundadora, near Matagalpa, at first tried to give equal pay for equal work in fertilizing the coffee trees and other tasks, he told me in June 1981. But the men insisted on being paid at a higher rate, threatening otherwise to work less.

Moreover, women do not get the higher-paying jobs, such as tractor drivers. Women typically have jobs such as cooking meals for the workers and cleaning out the administration buildings. When this fact is pointed out to (male) administrators and ATC leaders, they see it as "natural" because "the women don't know how to drive tractors." Conversations with women workers on a dairy farm near León made clear that they would like to milk cows and drive tractors but they also said that they didn't know how. Yet asked if they would like to learn, they unhesitatingly responded, "Of course!"

New Incentives

The Sandinista leadership has repeatedly stated—and shown —that it is determined to work out a mix of non-coercive means of motivating workers. "We are seeking to replace negative incentives with positive incentives," one Sandinista explained to me. A good part of the search is simply trying to get the workers to understand the importance of their work given the economic crisis in which Somoza left Nicaragua. On a state tobacco farm, the workers are reminded that their tobacco's quality is world renowned and they must work so that it doesn't lose its reputation. By contrast, the Somocista owners of that farm forced workers who performed poorly to stay for extra hours of unpaid work.

Recognizing that the drop in productivity can be related to the failure of workers to connect increased production and profits with improvements in the cash and social wage, the ministry is trying to open the farm's balance sheet to its workers. But to do this the ministry itself has had to develop farm-level accounting methods. In practice, if not in theory, the entire state sector was run out of one big purse during the inevitably chaotic first couple of years.

During the initial period of any true social transformation a drop in productivity is to be expected because workers will celebrate their freedom by rebelling against a history of exploitation in their workplaces. As the Sandinistas see it, eventually the workers will have new reasons to work, encouraged by a new form of authority—one coming from the workers themselves. By the end of the second year, this was beginning to happen. Augusto Zeledón, administrator of La Fundadora coffee plantation, told me in June 1981, "At first there was a lot of disorientation. Workers were coming two, three hours late and going off early to work their own plots. But now they are working practically a full day. What has made a difference is that I spend a lot of time talking to the workers in the fields. And the workers have gotten more organized and learned what they can do, especially through setting up and managing the store here."

Unlike their counterparts at similar periods of the Cuban and Chinese revolutions, the Sandinistas do not seem to be ideologically opposed to some linkage of wages (both cash and social) to increased productivity. In fact, a system of incentives perceptibly tied to advances in production and efficiency seems imperative. Workers themselves need to set norms of work—easier for some jobs than others—so that a schedule of incentives can be agreed upon, not imposed. An accounting system that everyone understands is also necessary to encourage increased efficiency as well as increased production. Questions about the types of incentives compatible with the goal of decreasing sharp inequalities among rural people—lest state farm workers become a labor aristocracy in the countryside—and the best balance between individual and group incentives are still being debated within the ATC and several ministries.

The challenge is to make the state farms profitable without resorting to coercion or exploitation of the people who work on them.

NINE

IS SEIZING THE LAND REVOLUTIONARY?

A BOVE ALL ELSE, THE POOR MAJORITY IN NIC-
aragua yearned for land—land to feed themselves,
land for security, land to free themselves from the humilia-
tion of having to sell their labor and even that of their children to a *patrón*.

By the last years of the Somoza dictatorship, well over
two-thirds of those working in agriculture had been either
totally deprived of land or deprived of enough land to support themselves. Since there was work on the plantations for
only three to four months of the year, 80 percent of the land-
poor Nicaraguans had to subsist "catch-as-catch-can." They
hunted small wild animals and harvested fruits with seasons
different from the export crops. They had their children beg
or peddle loaves of bread, flowers, or coconuts in the cities.
And they sold their labor power for an hour or a day at a time
to anyone who would buy it—anything to scrape together
enough money to survive until the next harvest season.

Their hopes for land were reinforced by the Sandinista slogan in some of the war zones: "Land for whomever works it!"
Land takeovers organized by outraged peasants were part of
the Sandinistas' strategy against Somocistas during the war.
But once they were in charge of the country's economy, the

Sandinistas had to confront the implications of a sweeping "land to the tiller" reform. Immediately the Sandinistas called for a halt to land takeovers. Their primary concern: if most of Nicaragua's rural people became landowners, would there be enough workers for the export plantations that generated 80 percent of the foreign exchange—foreign exchange now needed more than ever by a country devastated by war and deeply in debt? Moreover, if the Sandinistas did not discourage land takeovers, the big landowners controlling most of the export crop land would feel threatened and seek to liquidate their operations. The Sandinistas also feared that spontaneous land takeovers would result in thousands of tiny plots, too small ever to produce efficiently.

Reinforcing all this pragmatic reasoning was the belief of many Sandinistas at the start of the revolution that a wage-earning ("proletarianized") labor force represented historical progress. They felt it laid the foundation for eventual worker self-management. Thus increasing the number of peasants, especially individual small owners, would be a step backward. "There have been many agrarian reforms that in one stroke have handed over the land," Jaime Wheelock stated in 1979. "But this type of land reform destroys the process of proletarianization in the countryside and constitutes an historical regression."

Not surprisingly, the landless were confused. A Chinandega campesino summed up the bewilderment of many a few days after the July 19 triumph: "I don't understand it at all. One minute seizing the land is revolutionary and then they tell you it is counterrevolutionary."

In seeking to discourage land takeovers in the months following the triumph, the new government tried to improve wages and working conditions on private and state farms rather than redistribute land ownership. With hindsight, a privilege rarely granted to revolutionaries, it appears that the Sandinistas probably underestimated the depth and strength of the demand for land. For as the months went on, there were innumerable land takeovers, spontaneous as well as ATC-organized, especially of lands that had not been planted and where landlords refused to rent land at the new legal rates. The situation was especially tense in areas like the northern provinces, where the campesinos lived far away from most wage-labor plantation jobs and could barely survive on marginal lands rented from the big growers.

The fact that the Sandinista-allied association itself, the ATC, was involved in land seizures in some areas reveals a fundamental tension within the Sandinista Front in the early period: Is seizing the land revolutionary or counterrevolutionary?

The ATC, whose members were experiencing cases of gross injustice in the countryside every day, argued that land seizures represent the just, historic response of the rural majority. The Sandinista directorate, feeling responsible for the long-term survival of the revolution as a whole—lest all the gains of the rural majority be ultimately reversed as in Chile after Allende—tended to oppose postvictory land seizures. Of course, there were also ATC leaders who saw the "bigger picture," as well as top Sandinistas moved by the authentic popular demands. Once again, it was evident that agrarian reform was a never fully successful balancing act.

By early 1980 the conflicts over land seizures were moving inexorably toward a center-stage showdown. In late 1979 the courts moved to return to owners those farms and ranches spontaneously taken over by peasants and farmworkers, if it could not be proven that the owners had close ties to Somoza. For the ATC, however, *any* return of properties to private owners signaled a halt in the process of agrarian reform just when so many workers and peasants believed it should move forward.

On February 17, 1980, the ATC organized an unprecedented demonstration through the streets of Managua to the Plaza of the Revolution. Brandishing placards, banners, and machetes, over 30,000 campesinos and landless rural workers from every part of the country demanded that "not one single inch of land be returned." They also demanded measures against landowners who refused to resume production, pay the minimum wage, or carry out recently decreed improvements in working conditions and fringe benefits. It was clear that the Sandinista Front had made up its mind to side with these demands: a Sandinista Air Force plane was even called in to bring campesinos from some remote areas to the rally.

The Sandinista Front obviously supported the demonstration because it proved to any who still doubted that there was popular support for a further decree. Jaime Wheelock, Minister of Agricultural Development and a member of the directorate of the Sandinista Front, addressed the demonstrators: "We know that your demands are just, and this march gives us the confidence to advance and make further transformations." While Wheelock reiterated the need for the agrarian reform to proceed in an orderly fashion, avoiding "anarchic and spontaneous actions," he insisted that "there are elements among the landowners who must be hit hard if their lands are left idle. . . ."

On March 2, taking its legitimacy from such a groundswell of demand in the countryside, the government decreed that all lands taken over up to that time would remain in the public domain, the Area of the People's Property. Still, it was a balancing act: in recognition of the rights of private property, the former owners who could not be proven to be Somocistas would be compensated. Thus, in effect, the decree was an exercise in eminent domain. Farms belonging to small producers were exempted from the decree. And the government assured private landowners that further land takeovers would be strongly discouraged.

Workers and neighboring land hungry campesinos wanting part of the land to plant food crops put pressure on state farms as well as large private farms. At first, many state farm administrators refused these demands. They had two fears: loss of labor for the harvest and loss of land that might eventually be needed to expand production.

But as the pressure built, the ministry tended to give in, at least allowing the landless to "borrow" unused acreage on state farms, theoretically on a season-to-season basis. The workers had to pledge to work the land cooperatively and promise to work for wages on the state farm when they were needed. In fact, the peak seasons for work on the export crops and work on the staple food crops generally do not conflict. Many state farms did have more land they could effectively use; lending it to the landless helped deal with the unemployment problem in the countryside without increasing the total payrolls of the state farms. With the strong pressure for land in Spring 1981 and the all-out push to boost food production, lending idle state farm acreage became official policy. The land-lending policy enabled the government to make a stronger case against the big growers, for if the state farms were not using all their land, it was difficult to criticize private owners for keeping lands idle. The government also figured that its lending of idle land in exchange for an agreement to work when needed would automatically put pressure on many private landowners to do the same, since the large private farms and the state farms compete with each other for harvest workers. This pressure on the big private growers would also help meet the hunger for land.

Under pressure from the newly organized union of small and medium producers (UNAG), the government decreed at the same time that lands traditionally rented out, and idle lands, must be rented to the landless. Many landowners refused to obey the law, charging much higher rents than allowed in zones where there was a great demand for land, or planting pasture or sorghum rather than renting the land.

"We Won't Be Hungry Any More"

Just when many in the government hoped that there would be no more land takeovers, they picked up again as the time for the Spring 1981 planting of corn and beans approached. As campesinos told me, "with the smell of moist earth after the first rains, people yearn to have some land."

But this food crop planting season came at no ordinary historical moment. The new Reagan administration, sharply hostile toward the Nicaraguan government, abruptly cut off $9.8 million in credits for importing U.S. wheat, reinforcing the idea that Nicaragua must become self-sufficient in food production. At the same time, many commercial farm owners were leaving their lands idle and illegally liquidating their assets. From the ATC and UNAG in the field, as well as from the ministry itself, came repeated reports that many campesinos and farmworkers could no longer be talked out of seizing idle farmland. Peasants and workers were particularly outraged by the landowners who refused even to rent idle lands.

One such landlord was Adolfo Pastora, who planted only 85 acres of his 24,000-acre farm. Pastora often resided outside the country and repeatedly refused to rent land to any of the hundreds of nearby poor campesinos.

A group of these campesinos went to the local agrarian reform official to demand the land legally. The official told them, "You know that's against our policy of national unity. That is going to send a cold chill through every private producer in the country. Maybe we can find a way to give you a piece of land, but to expropriate all this—we don't want to do it." But the peasants were not persuaded, as they told me later. They told the official he was mistaken and that he should consult with his *jefe*.

Working with the ATC, they organized demonstrations in front of government offices in the nearby towns. In May 1981, 600 went straight to the head office of the agrarian reform in Managua. There they found Salvador Mayorga, the director of the agrarian reform who had worked with some of the campesinos during the liberation war. He heard them out, then agreed to order confiscation of the farm. The triumphant campesinos returned to the Pastora farm and started planting.

When I visited them several weeks after the takeover, their enthusiasm was evident. The sun shone down on their newly planted crops, their guarantee of plenty to eat in just a few months. Along with the new crops, there was an obvious new sense of self-respect. An old campesino, with deep wrinkles in his face, told me that since learning to read and write in the literacy campaign, "I don't bow down and conform any more. I used to hide, but now I stand up."

"We won't be hungry any more," said a woman with a child in her arms, pointing to some vegetables she'd planted nearby. Standing in a rough-hewn, smoky, communal kitchen, she told me about her life. At the age of twelve she had gone to Managua to work as a maid so that she could send money back to her family. "When my employer sensed the coming popular victory, he fled to Miami," she explained. "I returned to my family here in the country."

The next morning back in Managua, I picked up *La Prensa* and read the big three-inch headline: "Courts rule the Pastora farm should be given back." Adolfo Pastora had returned from abroad and hired some top lawyers. *Barricada*, the Sandinista afternoon paper, interviewed some of the same campesinos I had spoken with. One had told me of losing his thumb in an accident on the Pastora farm when he was 14 years old. Pastora refused to help him. "We will die before we give back one inch of this land," he told *Barricada*.

Less than three months later, the peasants were vindicated by the new agrarian reform law which made them legal owners.

TEN

A CONSERVATIVE AGRARIAN REFORM?

E VERY DAY FOR TWO YEARS THE PRESSURE
mounted on the government to come up with a comprehensive agrarian reform. Not only did many of the big
growers fail to use their land productively but some were also
draining money and productive assets from the country,
often with the help of generous government loans. From the
campesinos and seasonal farmworkers came an additional
pressure on the government to act: illegal seizures of idle
land by those outraged that good land lay unused while they
went hungry. By mid-1981, everyone in the country, rich
and poor alike, wondered when the revolution would enact a
land reform and what it would be like.

A year earlier Minister of Agrarian Development Jaime
Wheelock had assigned some key people in the ministry to
work day and night to draft a comprehensive agrarian reform
law. And on July 19, 1980, the first anniversary of the victory over Somoza, the government announced that the agrarian reform law was ready and would shortly be presented for
deliberation to the Council of State. But the law, though
drafted, was never presented.

A few months later, I asked ministry officials why the new
law had never been presented. The ministry was reluctant to
take on the administrative burden of expropriating a myriad

of idle properties, scattered here and there, I was told. There was, after all, enough idle land in the state sector, the vice minister for agricultural planning explained to me. "We need time to get our own act together first," he observed wryly.

I was also told that the ATC, the farmworkers' association, felt it hadn't had a large enough role in formulating the draft. It wanted a more flexible law.

More fundamentally, the big growers, lobbying through their producer associations, had objected to a land reform, *period*. And, as it became increasingly apparent that Ronald Reagan would be the new U.S. president, the Sandinista leadership put top priority on the broadest possible unity, anticipating heightened U.S. hostility.

There also seemed less urgency for the new law. The mere announcement of an impending law that would require owners to use their land productively, at penalty of losing it, had the effect of "motivating" many cotton growers to get on with the overdue planting of their fields, Vice Minister Salvador Mayorga told me. At the same time, the rural poor were seizing fewer farms and ranches because the main season for planting corn, beans, and other staples had passed. As the pressure waned, the draft law wound up on the revolution's back burner.

But just for the time being. During my visits to Nicaragua in the first six months of 1981, I found a clear acceleration of "decapitalization" and other forms of economic sabotage by many of the larger private producers. As a consequence, the rural poor grew increasingly impatient. They couldn't understand why the government didn't act to stop it.

The Sandinista leadership was responding, however. It was at work in the ministry, in the farmworkers association, and in the newly created small producers union (UNAG). Carefully and deliberately, they sounded out campesinos and large producer associations, farmworkers, administrators, and ministry workers around the country—all now enriched by two years of on-the-ground experience.

Then, on July 19, 1981, government and Sandinista leader Daniel Ortega read out the proposed Agrarian Reform Law to the applause of half a million Nicaraguans gathered to celebrate the second anniversary of the victory. The proposed law went to the Council of State where certain changes were recommended and then back to the junta which made it official in late August.

The law is pragmatic; some have even called it conservative. I've been told that many larger landowners had expected something "much worse." Virtually unique among land reforms, it places no ceiling on land ownership and emphatically reiterates the state's guarantee to protect the right to private property. But the law does set out once and for all the criteria and legal process for judging whether a landowner is meeting the obligation of ownership, making the land produce efficiently.

At the time the Agrarian Reform Law was announced, ministry officials estimated that perhaps as much as 4 million acres, roughly 30 percent of the country's agricultural land, was abandoned, idle, or inadequately used and therefore could eventually be redistributed.

In its provisions for redistribution, the law reaffirms the Sandinistas' commitment to a mixed economy in the countryside. Internal government projections are that in due course, as a consequence of the application of the law, 40 percent of the agricultural land will wind up belonging to independent campesino credit associations and production cooperatives, 25 percent to the state, 5 percent to small individual owners, and 30 percent to medium and large individual owners.

Large and even very large owners, however, are not excluded from the government's vision of the new Nicaragua. The obvious case in point is Sr. Pellas, the largest private landowner in the country, whose San Antonio complex produces almost half of the country's sugar and all the Flor de Caña export rum. He has no reason to fear expropriation for he has continued to invest his own capital, increasing both the area planted and total production. Pellas has been singled out for praise by the government on several occasions.

Since the law does not affect lands put to proper use, it will not shift any productive farms and ranches into new hands, a transfer which has disrupted production, at least in the short term, under other land reforms. Furthermore, production of food crops should be boosted by moving thousands of farmworkers, traditionally unemployed much of the year, onto fertile but idle lands.

At the same time, the government hopes the law will increase the production of export crops by the nation's commercial producers; the law sought to remove any uncertainties they had, thus hopefully encouraging them to invest. Many—some in blatant bad faith—had complained during the first two years that they could not commit themselves to producing or investing given their uncertain future. They complained that the government had not legally defined the role of private farming and was looking the other way when the poor took over idle or underused lands. Hanging over them was the knowledge that virtually all other Latin American revolutions had placed ceilings on land ownership— some even confiscating an *entire* property, not just the part exceeding the limit. The new law explicitly forbids land seizures by peasants and workers but also makes more precise the obligation of landowners to produce and sets forth the legal consequences of failure to do so.

Land Redistribution Under the New Law

Under the law, any abandoned land can be redistributed by the government. In such cases, there will be no compensation. Idle or underused land on very large holdings (over 850 acres in the prime Pacific Coast region; over 1,700 acres in the rest of the country) are also subject to expropriation. The total amount of land owned by one individual or partnership, regardless of how many separate farms, is used to determine the size of the holdings. Lands with titles transferred to other members of the same family are considered part of the same holding, thus short-circuiting a classic land reform evasion tactic. ("Idle" is defined as not cultivated for at least two years; "underused" refers to farms where less than 75 percent of the land suitable for farming is in use; cattle lands are underused if there is less than one head of cattle for each 3-1/2 acres on the Pacific Coast and for each 5 acres in the rest of the country.)

Making the acreage provision so generous indicates that the law does not target the medium size producer. The main targets of the reform are not so much big farms but large cattle haciendas that pasture relatively few cattle, often on prime cultivable land.

If only part of an estate is left idle or underused, the entire estate will not be expropriated, the law states. Only the neglected land will be seized. In one case, an owner was cultivating only 300 of 1,200 acres. The 900 idle acres were expropriated and given to a cooperative made up of nearly landless workers. The government then gave the owner a loan to irrigate the remaining 300 acres so he could increase production on that land.

Over the protests of farmworker and peasant organizations, the law prescribes compensation to owners for all idle or unused land taken over. However, owners caught decapitalizing (selling off machinery or cattle) will not be compensated.

The law also seeks to end the exploitation of poor farmers by absentee landowners. On farms larger than 85 acres in the Pacific Coast area and 170 acres elsewhere, any lands being rented for cash or labor or being sharecropped can be expropriated. The applicable farm size for rented land is set lower than for idle land because the poor tenant/absentee owner relationship is considered so unjust and economically backward.

But small farms are exempt. In some areas, truly small, poor farmers who work the land themselves also rent out part of it. While they will not be affected by this part of the law, it is hoped that in due course the agrarian reform will provide their tenants with their own land. The earlier decree placing a low ceiling on rent remains in force.

Of course, the government can expropriate very large farms that are entirely rented out to commercial producers, often the case with cotton plantations. In this case the government can opt to rent to the same producers but with the rent going for the public good rather than to an absentee landlord. The logic behind this decision is that unlike the actual operators of the rented cotton plantations, the absentee owners contribute nothing to production.

"The government is not dividing the people according to an abstract logic that often creates a tremendous amount of social conflict," Father Peter Marchetti, an American Jesuit rural sociologist employed by the Ministry of Agricultural Development, told us. "We are not going to expropriate the land of those who own, say, 200 acres, as was the case in Chile and in most other reforms which have set a limit on size. In this sense, the Nicaraguan land reform is much more just because it punishes only those who are parasites on the peasantry and on the society."

Even in compensating for expropriated land, the law recognizes differences among landowners. Landowners, whose land is taken over will be compensated according to tribunal judgments of how drastically they underused or destroyed the productivity of their estates and whether they did so out of neglect or to drain money out of the country. Those judged to have done the least harm will receive bonds at 4 percent interest that can be claimed in 15 years. The worst offenders will get bonds at 2 percent interest that mature in 35 years. An owner without other sources of income and unable to work will receive a pension of at least 1,000 córdobas a month.

Who Gets the Land?

Just as those who fail to produce are to be expropriated under the law, so the most industrious of the poor peasants are to be the first to receive land. Campesinos who banded together during the first two years of the revolution and have proven themselves responsible by obtaining good yields, working together in some form of cooperative, and paying back their loans from the bank, are to be the first to receive land titles.

Preference is also given to families of heroes and martyrs from the liberation war and to those who risked their lives. The next priority is impoverished small farmers who need more or better land just to meet their basic needs.

Preference is also given to those willing to organize themselves into some form of cooperative. The government's encouragement of credit associations and production cooperatives reflects its view that, at least in the longer term, cooperatives rather than scattered family farms can better take advantage of economies of scale. This includes not only for crop processing centers and other production facilities, but also social advances such as clinics and schools. But cooperatives remain voluntary. In fact, the first titles under the new law were awarded on World Food Day 1981 to individual families in the Wiwilí area, where Sandino had worked with the peasants over 50 years earlier.

Next in line to receive land are landless farmworkers. They are given lower preference because the government fears that once they have land of their own to cultivate food crops, they will be reluctant to work in the export crop harvests which are so critical for the nation's foreign exchange earnings. The ATC is organizing landless worker families into "Seasonal Worker Committees." These committees will report idle lands and organize themselves to receive and work them cooperatively. But they are also committed to making their members available for work in the export harvests when needed.

State farms have the next priority to receive newly expropriated lands. Putting state farms so far down the list reflects the view that the primary task is to get the already established state farms to function well as a modern, efficient pole of development before even thinking of expanding them. In some areas, especially those lightly populated, newly expropriated land might be combined with existing state farms to create more rational production units.

Minister Jaime Wheelock has stressed that state farms, like private farms, must live up to the production responsibilities that come with ownership. State farms that cannot prove themselves to be producing efficiently will, like private estates, be turned over to the landless and the land-poor. In the first year of the Agrarian Reform Law, over 300 state farms were turned over to campesino cooperatives and individual family farmers. In many areas, during the first year of the new law, most of the land titled over to peasants has been state land.

The lowest priority in land redistribution goes to the urban unemployed who want to return to the countryside to produce basic food staples.

The exact amount of land that agrarian reform beneficiaries will receive will vary according to the quality of land and local circumstances; the guideline is that the minimum acreage be sufficient to yield an income equivalent to the legal minimum wage.

Land titles granted under the law come free and unencumbered. By contrast, in many other land reforms the beneficiaries have had to pay for the land. The Nicaraguan agrarian reform titles cannot be sold; for this reason, opponents of the revolution, both inside and outside Nicaragua, have argued that the government is defrauding campesinos. But the government's intention is to forestall any new process of land concentration. And the land titles can be used as collateral for loans from the state banking system.

The agrarian reform is also designed to work against the land fragmentation so characteristic of rural misery in much of the Third World: while the land titles can be inherited, the land cannot be divided among heirs. Land received under the law can be transferred to a cooperative and, if none is adjacent, it is possible to exchange it for equivalent land suitably located to become part of a cooperative.

Rational Land Use

The new Agrarian Reform Law aims for more than greater justice in the use of Nicaragua's agricultural land; it also provides for more rational use of the country's agricultural resources. Under the Somoza system, rich soils, well-suited to growing crops, were usurped by powerful ranchers for grazing cattle, while peasant producers were forced to grow food crops on low-fertility, easily eroded hillsides suitable for grazing. An "agricultural development zone" provision of the law authorizes the agricultural ministry to identify the best agricultural uses of each productive area and to guide the appropriate commercial, peasant and state production to those uses. Such land use planning could not only increase production but also make easier government technical assistance to producers. Moreover, concentrating certain crops in certain areas will facilitate the efficient use of crop processing industries such as rice-drying plants.

A good example of the use of this provision of the law is a mammoth sugar cane development scheme in Tipitapa, not far from Managua (although investment in sugar cane is in itself controversial). Over five years, cane will be planted on 50,000 acres, half belonging to private owners. The projected state-owned mill will be the largest and most efficient in Central America, using only cane waste products for fuel and indeed generating a surplus of electricity. The project is slated to cost $250 million, with $103 million of that financed by Cuban government aid.

Implementation: The Hard Part Starts

A land reform which sets an arbitrary ceiling on landowner-
ship can be implemented virtually overnight; one that uses
efficient production as its criterion instead of size takes
longer. The Nicaraguan land reform, if it is to be effective,
requires careful case-by-case study: even then there will no
doubt be differences in judgment. The Sandinista leadership
has stressed that their agrarian reform will take years to implement. Since the law cannot be properly implemented
quickly, they hope there will be time for many "wait and see"
producers to realize they can live—indeed, can prosper—
with it.

If Nicaragua were land-scarce, the government might be
tempted to apply the new law harshly—redistributing land
whenever there was a shred of doubt about its productive
use. But the Nicaraguan revolution's great luxury is its overall abundance of land, so tremendous that even in the most
optimistic scenario about the performance of the larger landowners, it is hard to imagine there would not be enough land
to distribute to the landless and the land-poor. (In some
areas, however, they might have to be relocated to land elsewhere in the country).

"We plan to do it right, however long that takes us," the
Director General of the Agrarian Reform, Salvador Mayorga, told me shortly after the promulgation of the law. Implementation procedures reflect considerable concern for due
process. Yet at the same time they recognize the danger that
landowners might use the legal process to obstruct progress
indefinitely—a tactic that has stymied land reforms in other
countries. Such delays would undoubtedly provoke land seizures, thus placing the government in the ironic and politically untenable position of arresting the rural poor in the
name of the revolution's agrarian reform. Thus special courts
have been established to streamline adjudications. While
landowners have the right of appeal, final judgments are to
be handed down within thirty days.

For its implementation, the law established two new structures. First is the National Agrarian Reform Council, with
parallel regional councils to carry out the functions of the
national council on a regional level. The council sees that

studies to assess properties that might be affected are carried out in collaboration with the farmworkers' and small farmers' unions. Landowners are required to show evidence of their productivity. The council also identifies individuals and co-operatives capable of properly using confiscated lands. The national council is made up of top officials as well as tech-nicians of the Ministry of Agricultural Development and Agrarian Reform, the director of the National Finance Cor-poration, and representatives of both the farmworkers' asso-ciation (ATC) and the small and medium producers' union (UNAG). Interestingly, final authority in deciding whether an expropriation procedure should be set into motion rests with the national council; otherwise, it was feared, local ten-sions might make the land reform process either overly radi-cal or overly restrained.

The second new institution for implementing the agrarian reform is a system of agrarian reform tribunals to resolve any claims of injustice or irregularity as well as other disputes. A national tribunal supervises a network of regional tribunals. Members of the tribunals are appointed by the national gov-ernment and, from what I have seen, generally include a small farmer or farmworker.

In the first year of the Agrarian Reform Law, 242 proper-ties totaling approximately 400,000 acres and belonging to 94 families were affected. Somewhat over 60 percent of the land was expropriated because it was judged to be idle or un-derutilized. One quarter had been abandoned by the owners; the remainder was rented or sharecropped.

Of the 94 owners, 18 filed legal appeals. Six appeals were upheld and the council's decision overturned; the land was returned to the six owners. Of the land expropriated so far, titles have been distributed for only 40 percent of it, to some 6,503 campesino families, nearly all in credit associations or production cooperatives. Salvador Mayorga's explanation of this gap was that it takes more time to identify good benefici-aries, especially if the emphasis is on cooperatives, than to identify bad hacienda owners. "We're working on it, but we don't want a single beneficiary to fail," he told me. "So we won't be rushed—even by President Reagan."

ELEVEN

COOPERATIVE WORK: WILL IT WORK IN NICARAGUA?

ALONGSIDE THE STATE FARMS AND THE PRI-vate commercial growers, the Sandinistas are encouraging the development of cooperatives—gradually and voluntarily. For the Sandinistas, setting up cooperatives represents a vindication of the rural-based leader who fought to free Nicaragua from the U.S. Marines. Half a century ago in the mountains of Nicaragua, Augusto César Sandino started cooperatives among campesinos, cooperatives that Anastasio Somoza obliterated in 1932, the day after he had Sandino assassinated. The Sandinistas took their name—and considerable inspiration—from this hero.

Sandinista leaders offer a variety of reasons for the new government's promotion of cooperatives. Some are philosophical: working together is morally superior to working alone, which can foster selfish attitudes and the exploitation of others, including family members; cooperative ownership works against the emergence of conflicts based on growing differences in wealth. But for the most part, leaders I've talked to stressed practical reasons.

During the years of fighting against the dictatorship from guerrilla bases in the countryside, many Sandinistas witnessed the isolation and extreme deprivation of the Nicaraguan campesinos. Campesino families often live miles from other families. With few and very poor roads, many have no access to schools, clinics, churches or even the simple pleasures of social life among friends. Thus cooperatives are seen as one way of drawing people together to make possible at least a better, more social, life.

The new government also knew that developing Nicaragua's food potential required getting credit and technical help to the country's numerous campesino producers. The government wanted to set up stores selling basic goods throughout the countryside to give campesinos an incentive to produce. These monumental tasks would be possible only if the government could work with organized groups of small producers rather than with over 200,000 individuals.

Finally, the new government hoped that as Nicaragua developed it would be able to use agricultural machines, machines economically justifiable only if used on large holdings. If the countryside remained carved up into tiny plots, even small tractors would not make sense. Such an argument for cooperatives is not lost on the peasants: in conversations with countless campesinos I have found tractors high on their list of desires. And they readily appreciate the need to share a tractor with other small farmers. The Nicaraguan government has solicited donations of tractors; the Soviet Union has been the principal donor.

To many North Americans, cooperatives no doubt connote the kind of idealism that leads both to coercion and to the undermining of production. And these fears are hardly surprising: if one believes that people will not cooperate willingly and that individuals working solely in their own self-interest are always the most productive, then surely cooperatives are suspect. In addition, in such countries as Tanzania, coercion has been used in forming cooperatives.

Keeping these doubts in mind, I've asked many questions in studying the new Nicaraguan cooperatives. What forms will these cooperatives take? Is the model rigid or flexible? To what extent will it be imposed rather than simply encouraged? And does the concrete evidence from the first three years' experience indicate that cooperative production might work in Nicaragua?

The First Step: Credit Associations

One type of Nicaraguan cooperative, the Credit and Services Association (CCS), resembles farm cooperatives here in the United States in certain ways. In it, small farmers keep their land individually, but join together to purchase fertilizer, seeds, etc., in bulk and at a better price. Each member receives credit for production expenses individually but elected representatives pull together the information and negotiate with the government bank on behalf of the entire group. In fact, it's more of an association than a cooperative. The Sandinistas hope these credit associations will be "schools of democracy" where campesinos accustomed to living in isolation will learn to build communities and gain confidence in working together. These associations, they hope, will serve as stepping stones to cooperatives in which land is worked together and work animals and equipment pooled.

To encourage peasants to form these associations, the new government offered them credit on a priority basis and at a substantially lower rate than for individual small producers. Peasants responded: over 1,200 credit associations were registered in the first year.

In most, however, the cooperation revolved around obtaining bank credit and perhaps technical assistance. Other activities were as individualized as before. Thus when credit was restricted during the second year (with some first-year debts not paid back and less credit available), many of these associations virtually disappeared. During this period, I talked with a member of a credit association near Estelí from which many members had recently withdrawn: "I don't have the words to explain why we don't work well together," he told me. "It's a disease that goes way back, a lack of experience."

But not all of these associations fall apart. Not surprisingly, more are thriving in regions where peasants were more actively involved with the Sandinistas during the war against Somoza. They already have some experience in building organizations, and many of these credit groups see themselves as precursors of "real" production cooperatives. At a cooperative I visited in June 1981, the members had decided to pull down their fences so that they would gradually grow accustomed to the idea of working their lands together. This practice of "invisible fences" has since been encouraged with other associations in such "advanced" regions.

The farmworkers' association, the ATC, was charged with organizing these credit and services associations until the creation of UNAG, the union of small farmers and ranchers, in April 1981; the government agency PROCAMPO provided technical assistance. Those associations receiving fairly regular visits by ATC and PROCAMPO people have tended to become more solidified; the visits themselves bring about meetings and give legitimacy to the leaders. But the capacity of the ATC and the government to make such visits has been limited.

On the other hand, many campesinos have mistrusted ATC organizers with urban student backgrounds. Organizers were rushing things—trying to accomplish everything at once, one campesino told me.

The credit associations vary from place to place because campesino members adapted the general model to the way they wanted to do things. Some were formed by small landowners together with people renting land. One that I visited in Apantillo del Sabalar was started by 20 landless laborers who originally came together through their involvement in a Catholic Action group. They pressured the medium-size producers in whose harvests they worked to rent them cheap parcels of land here and there. After the members of this group formed an association and received credit, reaped an ample harvest, and repaid the loan, the small landowners in the area got interested, too. "They made many other people, especially small owners like us, interested in the cooperative and getting a loan from the National Development Bank," a small landowner told me. "So we joined the cooperative, too."

For over a year the landless and the small landowners worked in the same cooperative. Then a technician from the government PROCAMPO divided the group in two—one for the landless, the other for the small landowners. His move reflected the Sandinistas' belief that cooperatives can function best in the interest of their members when members have similar assets. If small landowners are mixed into the same cooperative with landless seasonal workers, Sandinista leaders fear, the small farm owners will tend to take control of the administration of the cooperative and skew credit and other services to their personal advantage. This often occurs because better-off campesinos are more experienced in dealing with outside agencies and in recordkeeping. The better-off landowners even tend to hire other members of the association. In time, the Sandinistas fear, the cooperative would become something of a corporation in which some of the members would stop working in the fields at all and non-member laborers would be contracted.

At another credit association on a 3,500-acre cattle ranch in Boaco, the members are essentially *colonos*, workers living on or near the hacienda. The hacienda owner lent the members 226 acres at no charge; in exchange the workers promise to work (for wages) on the hacienda when they have free time. Launched with only 26 members, the cooperative now has 38. To expand, it had to overcome some people's fear that joining the cooperative means indebtedness and the prospect of jail if one cannot repay a loan. This fear of debt also prevented some from taking their full share of available loans. Campesinos will undoubtedly be more inclined to take such risks if their confidence in the new government grows.

The leadership of this cooperative is optimistic; the growth in membership is proof it is making life better, the general secretary told me. Optimism was also evident in a member who declared: "Last year we didn't harvest any crops. Now we see some really good crops coming in. We're not going to perish." And the owner, who bought the cattle hacienda only a few years before the overthrow of Somoza, told me it was functioning better than ever. He supports the revolution and has not joined the big cattlemen's association in Boaco.

To the Sandinistas, the credit and services cooperative is both an end in itself—a way to facilitate production by getting farm credit to the small producers—and a stepping stone to cooperative ownership and work. We'll see over the coming years whether this evolution actually takes place.

Production Cooperatives

The Sandinistas are not merely waiting, however, for this evolution; they are actively encouraging peasants to begin working the land cooperatively in what they call Sandinista

Agricultural Communes (CAS). Even before final victory the Sandinistas had seen to it that lands taken by campesinos and workers (under 250 acres) were not parcelled up but worked collectively by 10 to 30 families.

In a CAS, the type of cooperative most favored by the Sandinistas, small farmers pool their land, equipment and animals. There are no govenment rules determining how a CAS is to be run: it has been up to the members themselves to set the norms for work and decide how to divide up what is produced. Generally the profits are divided three ways: first to the individuals according to the amount of work performed; second to community projects such as clinics, schools, or meeting halls; and third to capital improvements such as plows or a tractor.

Sandinista leaders hope that such genuine cooperatives will serve to reduce rural inequalities. Members generally share in earnings according to the work they perform without regard to the land or other assets they contributed in forming the cooperative, although some CASs have made exceptions. Moreover, workers hired to help out during peak periods share in earnings on the same basis as members.

But at this stage, few small farmers have opted to collectively work their lands. As one ATC organizer told me, even the word *colectivo* is enough to scare off most small owners. It's no surprise then that after the first three years of the revolution the entire country had no more than two dozen CASs formed by peasants who had been small landowners before the revolution. Very early the ATC and the ministry began to see that CASs were a long-term goal, not an immediate prospect. The leadership made it very clear that nothing should be forced.

Given the peasants' fears about pooling their land, it's understandable that most of the cooperatives now in operation were either formed before triumph where the Sandinistas were especially active in working with the small producers or made up of close relatives where a basis of trust already existed.

Tres Esquinas (Three Corners) near Estelí falls into both categories. Its eleven members cultivate 49 acres in common. Six "pulled up their fences," as they like to say, to put their lands together. They also decided to collectivize a

5,000-córdoba ($500) debt belonging to the member who had contributed the most land. But the members did not give up all their assets to the CAS. One kept 17 acres of pastureland, since only cropped land was included in the CAS; two others contributed oxen but kept cows for their private use. Five previously owned no land at all; three of these were sons of the most well-off member, the owner of the 17-acre pasture. Two others had been agricultural laborers, sometimes working for the landed members before the formation of the CAS.

Tres Esquinas is almost an extended family operation. Except for the two who previously had been laborers, all are related; the two ex-laborers were likely to marry into the family, I was told.

The elected general secretary of the CAS is the member who had had the most land. He had worked closely with the Sandinistas since 1973 (which is considered very early): his house sometimes served as a command post. The two laborers joined the Sandinista combatants at the time of the September 1978 insurrection. "We experienced the collectivization of the war itself," one of them commented.

This CAS has received a great deal of government backing in the form of technical advice, credit (a year after the triumph the cooperative was over 20,000 córdobas in debt) and access to purchase of inputs. The other CASs have probably received similar help.

The government has been flexible in encouraging cooperative farming. Finding small landowners resistant to pooling land, the government, through the ATC, has organized cooperatives of the formerly landless and land-poor farmworkers—primarily on rented land but, increasingly, on land belonging to state farms. State farm land is lent rent-free on a seasonal basis to those agreeing to work the land together. These cooperatives were also called CASs, but many in the ministry referred to them as "nongenuine CASs" to distinguish them from those composed of small landowners. For that reason, they were increasingly called "work collectives."

About 1,300 such work collectives were formed in the first year, despite the government's initial ambivalence. It feared that members with land to cultivate would no longer seek work in the export harvests so crucial to the country's balance of payments. But once the workers were on the verge of seizing land, the ATC decided to get involved to provide the best "orientation"—to encourage the workers to work the land together and share its fruits. However, the ATC has not been able to do in-depth work with many of the more than 1,300 such cooperatives, Edgardo Garcia, the young Secretary-General of the ATC, told me.

Of these 1,300, about two-thirds are on land rented from private owners under the new low rates; the rest are on land lent by state farms. Traveling around the countryside, I realized that probably no two are structured exactly alike because the members feel free to shape them as they see fit. In some, the land is truly worked cooperatively. In others—usually where the members had had their own plots as tenants and sharecroppers—the members worked as if they individually owned plots. But even in these cases there was a fair amount of shared work.

Each cooperative elects a president, a bookkeeper and a supply person. For the work in the fields, a leader is elected each year. Once elected, the leader discusses the work with everyone and group decisions are made; in the case of disagreements, the leader has the final say.

El Sol is a good example of how the government works to promote cooperative work on idle lands on state farms. El Sol is a cooperative made up of former agricultural laborers on a cattle hacienda that had been taken over from a Somoza associate and turned into a state enterprise. As soon as the hacienda was taken over by the ministry, the workers began demanding land to grow food for themselves. At first the ministry resisted; but then it realized that if it did not relent, the workers would simply seize the land and divide it up among themselves. To prevent this, the ministry offered to lend the land on the condition that it be farmed cooperatively.

While some were not initially in favor of working the land cooperatively, now they are generally pleased. Work is done collectively, with a government loan paying daily wages to the members, technically an "advance" on profits. Once the loan is repaid, the members plan to divide the harvest based on the number of days worked by each member, also figuring in work done by members' children. They are growing rice, beans and corn and expect not to have to migrate for seasonal wage work as in previous years. However, the members promised the ministry that when they were free they would work for the going wage during peak periods on the hacienda. Throughout 1980 the biggest complaint of the cooperative members was the uncertain, season-to-season arrangement with the ministry. The administrator of the hacienda was concerned that more pasture land will be needed as the cattle herd is rebuilt after the massive slaughtering by the Somocista owner. The CAS members were asking the ministry for barbed wire to fence off their land from the cattle. But the ministry fears a fence would de facto make the land concession permanent. (Many CASs on state farms, even without cattle, have sought to fence off their fields as a symbol of a permanent arrangement.) The harvest-to-harvest uncertainty also tends to inhibit the cooperative members from making long-term improvements on the lands. Eventually the government's decision to redouble its commitment to national food self-sufficiency convinced the ministry to more permanently cede idle lands to cooperatives formed by seasonal workers.

By the end of the first two years, there were officially 3,820 credit associations and CAS production cooperatives with a total of 62,359 members, comprising 53 percent of all small producers. Indeed, the Sandinistas were concerned that both types of cooperatives have been formed faster than the government's capacity to provide them with with basic productive services. In fact, all too many cooperatives failed economically for this reason.

Analyzing this experience, the ministry and the leadership of UNAG decided to select 150 cooperatives—half CAS and half credit associations—and strengthen them by making sure they were properly supported, especially with technical assistance and machinery. These cooperatives would also get priority in long-term improvements of their productive capacity, such as by irrigation installations. In early 1982, cooperatives were selected in each region of the country on the basis of the past two years' experience. Criteria included stability, profitability or reasonable potential for profitability, commitment to cooperative work, and, for the credit associations, evidence of a tendency to collectivize not only credit but also services. The leadership emphasizes, of course, that they will not abandon the other cooperatives; but, as one official told me in May 1982, "we want less hit-and-miss." They hope that these successful cooperatives will give a good name to cooperatives in general and thereby encourage other peasants, including small landowners, to form cooperatives, especially on the lands being granted through the new Agrarian Reform Law.

In sum, the Sandinistas are promoting cooperative work by making credit available on more favorable terms to small producers organized in some form of cooperative. And, wherever they can, they are making cooperative work a condition for the landless seasonal workers getting land. Campesinos and rural workers are generally responding, for they can see the benefits to themselves. But the government has been much less successful in getting small landowners to pool their land, because unless cooperatives are lent machinery by the ministry or a private farm, it is very difficult to explain the advantages of collective work. The capacity of a cooperative to accumulate the surplus needed for capital investments and community projects (schools, roads, clinics, etc.) probably seems too ambitious and thus too distant to be an effective incentive. The moral or social benefits of "learning to work together" are likely too vague to attract many poor peasants who have coped with a hostile environment for so long by minimizing their risks.

The Sandinistas' forms of persuasion have been positive, not punitive. They adhere strictly to their view that cooperative work must come about voluntarily. They seem willing to take the time for a gradual transition, experimenting with varying forms of organization. The Sandinistas see cooperatives as only one part of the rural economy, operating alongside individually owned private farms as well as state farms. The Sandinistas thus set themselves apart from revolutionary leaders in several other agrarian societies who, with the same high ideals, have sought a more uniform and rapid transformation by using force when necessary.

TWELVE

CORN AND BEANS FIRST

OUR BOOK *FOOD FIRST* EXPOSES HOW, IN SO many countries, more and more land and financial resources go to produce luxury crops for export while the production of local food crops is severely neglected, even in the face of widening hunger and growing national dependence on imported food.

By 1979 Nicaragua had become an extreme case in point. From the early 1950s to the mid-1970s, the agricultural land used to produce luxury export crops expanded almost 40 percent. By the 1970s, 90 percent of all agricultural credit was earmarked for export crops with virtually none for local food production. In 1955, Nicaragua imported 21,000 tons of grains; by 1978 this country of rich farmlands was importing over ten times that amount. What forces were behind these developments?

As dramatized in chapter two, the history of the Nicaraguan countryside has been the story of more and more people forcibly deprived of land. It is the history of more and more people denied decent-paying jobs or even year-round work. As elites took ever greater control over Nicaragua's productive resources, fewer and fewer people were able to grow food for themselves or earn enough income to buy the food they needed. In economic terms, they could not make "effective" their demand for food. With such great poverty, the local market for corn, beans, and rice was so weak that growing them never looked like a promising business. The well-off, moreover, craved American-style foods, some of which (notably wheat-based foods) could not be produced economically in tropical Nicaragua. (See Table 5, p. 100.)

Thus the land-controlling elites naturally saw their road to profits in producing luxury crops for foreign consumers and importing the status goods they desired. In the few instances when they did put prime lands into basic food crops, such as when world cotton prices were down, it was to produce corn and sorghum to feed cattle destined for the U.S. hamburger market. In sum, the logic of the elite-controlled economy was to ignore the basic needs of Nicaraguans in favor of producing for foreign markets. In the mid-1970s, almost 70 percent of the country's entire gross national product was in export production, in contrast to 10 percent for Mexico and 18 percent for Chile. Maintaining such an *economic* system required force, the *political* system of a military dictatorship.

Then the disenfranchised overthrew the dictatorship. No one could seriously expect the food situation of the majority of Nicaraguans to improve overnight. Indeed, at least in the short run, the prospects were alarming.

The liberation war itself compounded a "normal" food situation which was already desperate for many Nicaraguans. The final offensive happened to coincide with the period when the fields should have been prepared for planting corn, beans, and the other staple foods. In some areas I visited, campesinos told me that during the war they had eaten the seed saved for planting for fear of starvation. Food production was forecast to plummet 40 percent in the first harvests following the victory. Moreover, food stores in the war-ravaged cities had been stripped bare by looting and food prices in the markets jumped 50 to 100 percent in the final months.

With victory, the revolution brought new jobs, higher wages, new money throughout the countryside through campesino credit, and cuts in rents for land and for urban housing. These programs directly and indirectly released some of the pent-up demand for more food. In fact, during the first

18 months following victory, the demand for food leapt a phenomenal 45 percent.

How was the new government to cope? It was determined to abolish hunger from Nicaragua and aware that for many Nicaraguans "the revolution is measured through the plate of beans." In this chapter we examine its efforts to improve the distribution of food, the supply side of the problem.

In the short run, the only solution was to import—massively and quickly—before speculation could drive prices even higher. While some countries, principally in Western Europe, donated food, a tremendous amount had to be purchased on credit. In the first few months, more food was imported than in the whole year preceding the war. In 1980, the beans and corn imported from the United States equalled almost a third of what was produced locally. The cost in precious dollars was staggering.

At the same time, the government sought to increase peasant production of corn and beans by an unprecedented offering of credit and by decreeing sharply lower rents for tenant farmers, most of whom produced corn and beans.

Yet there was a strong tension within the new government which I noticed during my first visit after victory. Since I was known as the coauthor of *Food First*, everyone assumed I would advocate priority to local food production. But many in the government worried that policies encouraging peasant food production—making it easier to get land to farm, cheap credit, technical assistance, and good reliable prices—would undercut export production as the poor majority in the countryside found it no longer needed to work in the export harvests. "Food First" policies, they feared, would reduce the country's ability to earn dollars just when dollars were needed more than ever to pay off the Somoza debt, to pay for imports vital to reconstruction, and to pacify the potentially counterrevolutionary well-off classes accustomed to imported consumer goods.

Others stressed the sad shape of local food production and wanted to focus attention there. In the agricultural year 1980-81, bean production had fallen to two-thirds of what it had been in 1977-78, while corn production showed virtually no increase.

Throughout 1980 and into 1981 the food debate roared on. Sometimes it seemed there were as many viewpoints as there were participants; yet none was simplistic. To reach a resolution, research was carried out; developments internally and internationally were continually evaluated. In March 1981, shortly after a major consultation with about two dozen of us foreign advisors (no Cubans, no Soviets!), a rough consensus emerged within the Nicaraguan leadership. Ironically, it was the Reagan administration that brought deliberations to a dramatic conclusion. For at the beginning of April the Reagan administration abruptly canceled a $9.8 million loan to import wheat from the United States. Only days later the Nicaraguan government unveiled a major comprehensive program for achieving food self-sufficiency; all the ministries involved were instructed to give the program top priority.

Indeed, a prime motive behind the program is national independence. For as long as Nicaragua is dependent on food imports, its national sovereignty stands in jeopardy. This was especially true since in the first two years most food imports came from the United States, the country which has repeatedly intervened directly in Nicaragua's affairs, and from other Central American countries whose elite-controlled governments were increasingly belligerent toward the Nicaraguan revolution.

And there were other considerations. Nicaragua found that beans, the daily food of all Nicaraguans, were hard to find on the international market. Countries with far greater financial power than Nicaragua—Mexico, Venezuela, Brazil—corner much of the world market in beans. Beans purchased from California and Texas were expensive and, worse yet, were simply not to the liking of Nicaraguans, who insisted on their locally grown *frijolitos rojos*. A similar situation prevailed with corn. Nicaraguans are accustomed to *white* corn, which commands a premium on the world market. Oil-rich Venezuela is the major buyer of white corn and the major supplier is South Africa, a country whose government is hardly likely to be a dependable ally.

Moreover, the government found study after study projecting that international prices for grains and other staples were likely to rise significantly faster than those for Nicaragua's traditional exports: coffee, sugar, and cotton. Thus ever more cotton would be needed to buy a ton of corn or beans. In addition, if decent wages were to be paid while exports of cotton, sugar, and coffee remain competitive in world markets, expensive technology to increase labor productivity would have to be imported. Pesticides, fertilizers, and other imported materials already represented almost 40 percent of cotton production costs (while corn and beans were produced with virtually no foreign exchange costs). Finally, cyclical overproduction problems for cotton, coffee, and sugar result in periodic sharp drops in international prices and in marketing quotas.

Calculations indicated that on only 60 percent of the amount of prime land being used to grow the cotton that earned the dollars to import beans from the United States, it would be possible to raise the same quantity of beans—and they would be Nicaraguan beans grown in Nicaragua. Indeed, once domestic needs are secured and every Nicaraguan can afford an adequate diet, Nicaragua might well be able to export beans, white corn, and grain-fed poultry and hogs on better terms than its "traditional" agricultural exports. This capacity to generate foreign exchange for the nation could, in turn, give new prestige to campesinos, traditionally the most disparaged group in Nicaragua.

The Sandinistas also understood that making food production a priority would entail greater government support for campesinos. That in turn would help to build greater support for the overall revolutionary program among the biggest producer class in the nation.

Nicaraguan policymakers began to realize that "food versus export crops" was partly a false dilemma. Nicaragua could *both* produce more food for local consumption and more for export. It could increase its exports of coffee, sugar, beef, and cotton primarily by using the lands already devoted to their production more efficiently and fully. In addition, Nicaragua could increase food production by providing more support and better prices for peasant producers as well as by allowing peasants and seasonal laborers to plant on idle lands (as provided under the new agrarian reform law).

Fears about whether there would still be a sufficient labor force for the export crop harvests began to wain as policymakers realized that since peak work periods for corn and bean cultivation generally do not coincide with those for export crops it should be possible to work out agreements by which, in exchange for access to land, landless workers and campesinos would agree to work when needed in the export harvests (for decent wages and under ever improved conditions).

Thus in April 1981, a national food plan to achieve food self-sufficiency as soon as possible was unveiled. The initials of the Programa Alimentario Nacional, P.A.N., conveniently spell the word for bread in Spanish. (Some might say it is ironic that P.A.N. means bread since Nicaragua, for climatic reasons, cannot be self-sufficient in wheat.) From the beginning the government stressed that this was a very special emergency program requiring a national mobilization. Media, posters and speeches proclaimed: "Food is a priority."

But how would P.A.N. achieve its goal? From the start, the program stressed that food self-sufficiency means more than eliminating most food imports through improved local production; it also means assuring every Nicaraguan an adequate diet. As we stress in *Food First*, many governments in the world have claimed to be self-sufficient in food while the majority of children went hungry. Thus the program encompasses both increased production and more efficient and just distribution. The distribution side we will discuss in the next chapter; here we focus on the production side of P.A.N.

First of all, P.A.N. goes all out to motivate and support small farmers, traditionally the principal suppliers of the nation's staple foods (except rice, 60 percent produced on large mechanized farms in the state sector). But how? Studies of the first two years showed that better credit was not the best way to increase production. Raising guaranteed prices to producers was tried instead. The Somoza regime had favored low prices to campesinos, encouraging their exploitation by middlemen, so that campesinos would be forced to seek work in the export harvests. Keeping food prices low also allowed plantation owners to pay lower wages, giving them fatter profits.

Under P.A.N., the price paid to farmers for corn was hiked 25 percent; the price for beans, Nicaragua's most critical food, was boosted 50 percent. (These prices are still lower than those in other Central American countries.) The bean price represents a considerable savings over spending dollars to import U.S. beans.

At the same time it raised the guaranteed producer prices, the government committed itself to improving the rural distribution of consumer items such as kerosene, sugar, cooking oil, clothing, and radios at reasonable prices. Good crop prices are somewhat meaningless to Nicaragua's remote small farmers unless there are things they can buy with the money they earn, P.A.N. planners had learned. Indeed, better prices would be cancelled out by inflation if there were not a simultaneous improvement in the supply of consumer good for purchase. Government credit to individual small producers and peasant cooperatives would continue at favorable interest rates, but it would be distributed with more care. For instance, credit would be distributed less as cash and more as production inputs, such as fertilizers, seeds, and tools. Clearly this will be easier with small farmers organized into cooperatives than with individuals on scattered, isolated plots.

The new Agrarian Reform Law, passed only four months after the launching of P.A.N., also promoted P.A.N.'s production goals. Under the new law, idle lands on both state and privately owned commercial farms and ranches can be turned over to peasants and landless seasonal workers, who invariably plant food crops. These lands are generally more fertile than those onto which most of Nicaragua's food producers had been pushed by the expansion of elite-controlled plantations. Thus the ministry hopes that average yields for food crops, pitifully low for so long, will be boosted even without costly imported chemical fertilizers (which are difficult to distribute in remote areas). At the same time, ministry agronomists have concluded that cotton is ruining some of the poor soils which the cotton entrepreneurs cultivated. And since a considerable number of larger cotton growers have been showing themselves unwilling to plant their estates fully, it seems sensible to restrict the total cotton acreage to soils that can best withstand cotton cultivation. The government thus could hand over to peasant cooperatives land better suited to food crops, land more fertile and more accessible to urban markets than the interior, hilly land onto which the expansion of cotton pushed so many campesinos.

P.A.N. also recognizes that producing more is not the only way to increase food availability. Of the country's corn crop, 30 to 40 percent is typically destroyed after harvest because of poor storage. So a government program is now teaching small producers how to built rat-proof, air-cooled corn cribs made from local materials, principally bamboo and thatch. They can be built in two to five days with little or no cash outlay. First 500 campesinos learned the new technique. Then each was to teach ten more campesinos so that by the end of 1981 the knowledge had theoretically spread to 5,000.

General observation in the countryside, even in the more remote areas, suggests that these pro-small producer policies mean that food producers themselves are eating better. Many campesinos have told me they are now raising more chickens and pigs so that they can eat better and boost their cash incomes. Under Somoza, ironically, they were among Nicaragua's worst fed.

Shifting Tastes

Achieving food self-sufficiency also involves reorienting eating habits toward foods that can be locally produced. The clearest example of this is the campaign to consume corn as opposed to wheat, which flourishes only in temperate climates and therefore must be imported. (Experiments are going forward, however, to cultivate wheat in one highland region. Apparently the campesinos there used to grow some wheat but the tradition was lost with the steady stream of wheat imports from the United States.)

Building on widespread public indignation with the Reagan administration's sudden cutoff of wheat credits, the government organized a series of corn festivals throughout the country. The theme was "Corn, our roots." (As with many slogans, this one translates poorly. The rhyming Spanish version is "El maiz, nuestra raiz.") The festivals did catch the imagination and national pride of the people. The symbol of the festivals was the indigenous corn god, Xilem. Cooking contests were held throughout the country for a whole range of corn-based foods, including tortillas and tamales as well as corn-based beverages, both alcoholic and nonalcoholic. Local winners were sent to a national corn cookoff in Masaya, where winners were awarded a trip to Corn Island, a Nicaraguan possession in the Caribbean complete with white sandy beaches. Even Sandy's, the local rival of McDonald's, got into the act, producing a "tortiburgesa," or corn tortilla burger.

If corn is "in," the government would like to see beef "out"—or at least "down." Beef exports, the third most important source of foreign exchange, fell dramatically in 1980 in part because Nicaraguans ate more beef. The government would like to see more people eating fish instead. Nicaraguans have traditionally eaten fish, but a low catch and inadequate distribution has limited consumption. The government's plan is to make loans to fisherpeople to buy boats, tackle and outboard motors. As with small farmers, these loans are being used to encourage cooperatives. By 1980, 26 new cooperatives were already producing 25,000 pounds of fish a month. A transport system is being organized to get fresh fish efficiently to market in Managua. In the Somoza days, fishing families would send one of their members to the capital by bus to sell the previous day's catch. Given notoriously fickle fish prices, sometimes these sellers would not even recoup their costs.

Even in its efforts to feed Nicaraguans better the government is meeting U.S. hostility. In early 1982, the United States blocked a $30 million loan from the Inter-American Development Bank to improve Nicaragua's fishing capacity and marketing.

Poultry and eggs are also seen as good beef substitutes. The war left the country practically stripped of small livestock, so in 1980 chickens were imported in an effort to boost animal protein consumption without reducing beef exports. But so many chickens were imported that the scheme was almost self-defeating. The cost turned out to be only $1 million less than the total earned from beef exports. Great effort has gone into rebuilding local poultry production, which can be significantly increased in months, compared to years for cattle. And in comparison to cattle, chickens are efficient converters of corn.

Efforts to introduce cultivation of soybeans and consumption of soy foods have also been one of the focuses of P.A.N.'s plan to improve the nutritional well-being of the Nicaraguan people.

The P.A.N. program in the countryside got off to a late start for the 1981 major planting season because coordinating all the ministries took longer than anticipated. Still, when the 1981 harvests started coming into the market in early 1982, it looked like P.A.N. was working. Bean production—perhaps the principal focus of P.A.N.—more than doubled, to a level considered self-sufficient *despite* a 40 percent increase in national consumption. Corn production, however, went up less than 9 percent, probably somewhat less than the nation's need; corn consumption has increased 35 percent since the victory. Unfortunately, the unprecedented floods in late May 1982 wiped out a considerable amount of the stored corn harvest, leading the government to import corn in the second half of the year.

For many, these results confirmed the thesis that boosting producer prices was key: bean prices had been increased much more than those for corn. Reports from some areas indicated that campesinos got credit for corn but then, except for producing their household corn needs, switched over to bean production; or, instead of marketing their corn, they fed more of it to their pigs and chickens. In response to the first year's results, before the 1982 planting season the government announced a greater increase in the corn price than the bean price.

Rice production increased 45 percent—almost double the production of the last year before the liberation war. This means that Nicaragua has achieved self-sufficiency in this third basic food. Only the shortage of warehouses prevents the country from becoming a net exporter of rice, a deficiency which an $11 million project with Mexico is designed to correct. Sorghum production reached a level more than double the last year before the war, more than sufficient for the nation's needs.

Poultry production was estimated by mid-1982 not only to have recuperated from the war but to have risen some 20 percent above the historical record. Egg production also showed sharp increases and by mid-1982 stood 30 percent above the prewar record. It was, therefore, possible to cut egg imports by two-thirds in the first six months of 1982 compared to the previous year, with every prospect of soon eliminating egg imports altogether despite greatly increased consumption.

Self-sufficiency has thus been achieved in several key food staples and near-term prospects are very encourgaging for most others. By 1982, the third anniversary of the triumph, many Nicaraguans could take satisfaction from their country's dramatic advance toward the national goal of self-sufficiency in basic foods—no small achievement, especially during a time of significant increase in national food consumption. But what about the other goal of P.A.N., that every Nicaraguan have an adequate diet? This is the question for the next chapter.

THIRTEEN

CAN THE FREE MARKET FEED THE POOR?

N ICARAGUA COULD IMPORT VAST QUANTI-
ties of food. And it could increase its food production,
even achieving self-sufficiency. But it could still fail to eliminate hunger. Because for poor people who don't grow their
own food, getting enough to eat depends on whether the
price of food is within their reach.

Confronting what looked like a potential famine at the
end of the war, the new government dramatically stepped up
food imports. World prices were steep and, still worse, had to
be paid in dollars. If these real costs were passed on to the
local food market, the poor majority would suffer. Many
might actually starve. No doubt that is what Somoza would
have done, but for the Sandinistas it was unthinkable. So
the government chose to subsidize massively the cost of food
imports and to forestall speculation by importing enough to
fill the markets for everyone.

Under this strategy, the government was footing the food
bill not only for the poor but for the middle classes and even
the rich. In fact, since the better-off could afford greater
quantities of food, they were disproportionately subsidized.
Any visitor to Managua in those days would have been struck
by the Inter-Continental Hotel's world class, all-you-can-eat
buffet of largely imported foods for $1.75. Subsidized imports

were obviously a very indirect and thus costly way to help the poor majority.

But could the new government have helped the poor majority more directly? Limiting the amount of cost-subsidized foods a person coud buy or making it available only to the poor would have been much less expensive for the government. But any such system would instantly have been labeled "rationing." And the word "rationing" strikes fear in Nicaraguans, including the poor. For years Somoza's U.S.-aided propaganda drummed in the message that rationing is the first foothold of "godless communism." Photographs of Nicaragua's well-stocked supermarkets were repeatedly contrasted with Cuba's drab ration books. No one from the Somoza regime, needless to say, pointed out that the majority of Nicaraguans couldn't afford to buy from Managua's supermarkets, while every Cuban was ensured at least a minimum basic diet.

During my visits to Nicaragua I often ran up against this fear of "rationing"—even though Nicaragua, unlike the United States during World II, never had rationing. I'll never forget a meeting with about 20 women from Ciudad Sandino, Nicaragua's largest working class barrio. In discussing their food problems, several poor women complained bitterly that the better-off in the barrio bought more food than they needed, hoarded it, and thus created shortages for others. There should be a fairer way of doing things—maybe cards or books where what each family buys could be recorded, they told me. "But," they emphasized, shaking their fingers, "we wouldn't want rationing."

Aware that poor Nicaraguans identify rationing with a lack of freedom, the Sandinista leadership from the start ruled out rationing, even of a single scarce item. After all, just what the U.S. government wanted Nicaraguans to believe was that Nicaragua was going to become "another Cuba." One day the Minister of Domestic Commerce was discussing with some of us foreign advisors the problem of the run on sugar supplies, supplies that theoretically were sufficient for all. "I was told I could do whatever I wanted to deal with the shortages, just as long as I didn't even mention the word 'rationing,'" he confided.

But the new government also ruled out rationing for prac-

tical reasons. The country's food is distributed by an unbelievable number of small vendors. (Managua's principal
market alone had almost 10,000 small retailers!) Admin-
istering a rationing system with so many outlets would have
been a nightmare for even the most experienced government.
With rationing ruled out, the government set its sights on
several other measures to improve the poor's access to food.
First, more jobs. During its first year, the government succeeded in cutting the unemployment rate in half—down to
17 percent. (Unfortunately, the new jobs were mainly in
government and other service occupations which did not increase the supply of goods. The new jobs therefore worked
against efforts to cut inflation.)
Second, higher wages for the working poor. The new government decreed a 125-córdobas-per-month raise for all those
earning less than 1,300 córdobas. A household income survey at the time indicated almost 40 percent of the urban
population should benefit. (To give you an idea of the potential impact on a poor family's diet, the "suggested" retail
price at the time for corn (kernels) was 1.15 córdobas a
pound; beans and rice 2.85 córdobas a pound each; and one
egg for 1 córdoba.)
Third, lower prices for other necessities. Housing rents
were sliced in half, and tranportation, education, and medical costs were strongly subsidized, all to release more of a
family's income for food. Finally, taxes on food were removed,
while taxes on alcoholic beverages were raised.

Entering the Marketplace—On the Side of the Poor

The Sandinistas shunned the idea of policing the prices
charged in the marketplace, a high official of the Ministry
of Planning, himself not a Sandinista, told me in October
1979. After all, he pointed out, they had risked their lives to
free a country terrorized by police. Besides, many of Nicaragua's food vendors were poor people and thus among the
very people the Sandinistas most wanted to help. Moreover,
he added, they had been warned against replacing market
mechanisms with "bureaucratic socialism" by no less an authority than Fidel Castro.
What should they do? Could they maintain the private

marketing of food and yet be sure that the market would at least respect the needs of Nicaragua's poor majority? The Sandinistas decided to try. At the heart of that experiment would be the National Basic Foods Corporation, ENABAS, set up just two months after the fall of the dictatorship.

ENABAS was to work with both small food producers and with poor consumers, and to do so without excluding private merchants.

To help food producers, ENABAS offered guaranteed prices for their crops, calculated to ensure them a decent profit. Historically, the smaller farmers, backbone of the nation's food production, were at the mercy of local moneylenders and itinerant middlemen who offered them low prices at harvest—taking advantage of the fact that most had no storage facilities and no way to get their crops to market. These middlemen then resold at a high mark-up to large wholesalers who sometimes hoarded the food to make even higher profits as supplies tightened on the retail market. With ENABAS in the picture, it was thought, middlemen would have to offer better prices, prices at least equal to those offered by ENABAS.

To help consumers, ENABAS would store up enough of the supply of basic foods so that whenever private merchants speculated on rumored shortages or hoarded, it could release enough onto the market at a low and stable price to undercut speculators, without resorting to policing. By "capturing" 40 percent of the total supply of basic foods, ENABAS could "keep the market honest," or so planners thought. If for some reason ENABAS was unable to purchase locally enough foods to protect consumers in this way, it had the authority and the dollars to import.

And, to prevent exports of locally needed foodstuffs, ENABAS was also granted sole authority to export them. Exporting in spite of local needs is a temptation to private producers and merchants since corn and beans fetch higher prices in Honduras and Costa Rica than in Nicaragua.

All of these plans for a government role in new Nicaragua's food system appeared to be a sensible way to begin to right centuries-old injustices. But how has ENABAS done in practice?

Helping Producers

Largely due to the government's overall inexperience, ENABAS' efforts to boost food production showed little success during its startup year. In chapter six, we describe the disappointing results in boosting food production through "spilling credit" in the countryside. But what turned out to be an even bigger disappointment for ENABAS was the difficulty in *purchasing* enough of what was produced, despite the fairly large corn crop in 1980.

While shooting for 40 percent, ENABAS was able to acquire only about 12 percent of the 1980 corn and bean crops. One reason was that ENABAS suffered a tremendous handicap compared to private traders: in payment, it offered only checks—something never before seen by most peasants. Private buyers offered not only cash but the goods campesinos needed but could not produce themselves: salt, sugar, kerosene, machetes, boots, cooking oil, and so on. ENABAS learned the hard way that an essential part of buying from small producers is selling to them, since many goods are hard to find in the countryside.

Even when campesinos were willing to sell, ENABAS often did not have the staff to handle the purchase, sorting, and transport of millions of pounds of grain. Transportation was a major bottleneck, especially with corn. Over three quarters of the corn harvest comes from the interior of the country, where roads are at best passable only during the dry season in some areas. Corn, harvested in October, could not be brought to market in many areas until the dry season started in February. And with so much credit available and so much grain to transport, the price of mules and trucks quickly shot up. Even where there were roads suitable for trucks, ENABAS often lacked the trucks. It had only 38, when it estimated it needed 218. To try to bridge this gap, ENABAS rented trucks from private owners at high prices or borrowed trucks from other government agencies.

ENABAS' prices to producers posed still greater problems. Figuring out a fair nationwide producer price—one that would cover all the producer's costs plus allow for a decent profit—is a very tricky business. How do you anticipate the inflation in costs, in part due to the flood of credit hitting the countryside, and the varying yields in different areas and for different size producers? While the government wanted the price to be high enough to help the peasants improve their standard of living in relation to urban dwellers, it feared setting prices so high that consumer prices would have to be massively subsidized lest the poor be cut out. On top of all this, ENABAS found itself limited as a bureaucracy trying to compete with much more flexible private buyers.

Take the case of beans. Beans are the number one food crop of Nicaragua since *all* Nicaraguans want their daily *frijolitos*. Thus they are a food for which the better-off and the poor compete directly. In 1980, rains at the wrong time and a pest outbreak destroyed 20 to 30 percent of the crop in one key bean-producing region. Rumors of a bean scarcity set off a consumer scramble. And private traders appeared in full force in the countryside offering up to 500 córdobas per hundredweight; ENABAS could hardly compete with its price set at only 220. (In some areas the Sandinista-led ATC expended precious political capital with the campesinos trying to persuade them that the "correct" thing to do—"for the sake of the revolution"—was to sell to ENABAS at prices well below what they could be getting. Much to its dismay, the government felt compelled to forcibly stop some campesinos from trying to take their beans across the border into Honduras, where bean prices were much higher.)

ENABAS also failed that year to get the corn it wanted, but for different reasons. With so much credit and exhortations to increase food production, many campesinos planted lots of corn. But with the inflated costs—due to the rush for scarce inputs—and yields below government projections, many campesinos found the ENABAS price of 80 córdobas per hundredweight would not even cover the rent for mules to take it to ENABAS. So they declined to sell to the ENABAS buyers when they came around, hoping for better prices later from private buyers. In the end, the corn harvest was abundant, and ENABAS imported so much corn, that prices offered by private merchants plummeted to 50 córdobas. At that price, many decided that it wasn't worth harvesting more of their crop than they could eat or feed to their pigs and chickens.

To fight the speculation set off by the scarcity scare in the marketplace, ENABAS repeatedly imported great quantities of corn, beans, and other foods, especially during its first year. Administratively, importing was immensely easier than purchasing locally. But, as pointed out in the previous chapter, the costs were exorbitant and national security was jeopardized. In addition, especially with the beans, people complained that they did not like the imported varieties.

Looking ahead for the 1981–82 season, ENABAS thought it had learned some useful lessons. For one thing, to compete better with private buyers it would have to substantially raise the price it offered to producers. In addition, as part of P.A.N., the National Food Program, ENABAS would try to stimulate sales by seeing that campesinos could buy the basic goods they wanted (from farm tools to sugar to transistor radios) at nonexploitative prices.

To avoid expanding its fledgling bureaucracy, ENABAS would work through established merchants with good reputations instead of opening a network of government stores. These private outlets would get government credit as well as help in securing farm and consumer goods at the official wholesale prices. The "honest" merchants would be identified by UNAG, the union of small and medium farmers and ranchers. Thus the Sandinista-led government has been working to shift the responsibility for coordinating rural credit, farm input delivery, the purchase of crops, and sales of manufactured goods to rural producers into the hands of experienced local merchants with good reputations. The idea is to work *with* the market, not against it, and thus avoid creating a large, inexperienced government bureaucracy, however well-intentioned.

Nevertheless, *frijoles* has persisted as problem *numero uno* for ENABAS—and therefore for Nicaragua's urban poor. Bean production doubled in 1981-82, apparently mainly in response to the much higher ENABAS-guaranteed price. But ENABAS has painfully learned that there are beans and there are beans.

For starters, Nicaraguans crave only the local (*criollo*) variety of red beans, even though some others are grown in Nicaragua and are generally easier to cultivate. (Black beans, much in demand by Brazil and some Caribbean countries, could be more easily produced in Nicaragua than the prized red beans, but Nicaraguans generally do not like black beans.) On top of this, beans of whatever variety vary in size, moisture content, firmness, and the amount of extraneous matter, like pebbles, mixed in. Considering all this, many campesinos sell their red beans and other good quality beans to private merchants for higher prices and then unload their "rejects" onto ENABAS. As if that's not bad enough, ENABAS has had difficulty properly drying and storing the beans (no doubt compounded by the lower quality of the beans), thus making its beans still less desireable.

In the marketplace and even in lunch counters, you will find people distinguishing "beans" and "ENABAS beans," and commonly paying more than twice as much for the non-government beans. So the poor majority winds up either paying through the nose for the beans they really want (and thus sacrificing something else they need) or they eat second-class beans. It's all politically costly for the government since every trip to the marketplace and every meal makes the government's logical constituency—the poor majority—more willing to listen to those who are out to discredit the revolution. For its part, the Sandinista government has been quick to publicize the real bean shortage in Costa Rica and the numbers of Costa Ricans coming into Nicaragua to buy beans.

Helping Consumers

While ENABAS fell far short of its goal of purchasing 40 percent of the basic foods produced in the country in 1980, it did succeed in becoming the wholesale supplier of 40 percent of most of the basic foods sold. It did so, of course, by importing. While this clearly was not ideal, at least ENABAS was in a position to be able to help poor consumers by deterring consumer price speculation, or so planners thought.

From the start the new government had hesitated to set consumer price ceilings for food items, fearing this might act as a disincentive for the country's food producers. But as more and more wholesalers and retailers took advantage of consumers by speculating on food prices, the government decided it had to act. Otherwise, all the measures designed to help the poor majority would come to naught. So in 1980 it set wholesale and retail price ceilings on 23 basic items, including beans, corn, rice, cooking oil, sugar, milk, soap, salt, and toilet paper. The prices of 50 other items were to be monitored in an effort to detect speculation and hoarding. From time to time over the next two years other items were added to the controlled list.

To allow retailers to make a sufficient profit, the plan was that ENABAS would supply them (as well as private wholesalers) at wholesale prices allowing for a retail profit margin. Priority attention was to go to retailers in poor neighborhoods.

While ENABAS was planned to help stabilize and keep down consumer prices primarily by operating as a wholesaler, it also developed its own retail network. That network's most important component consists of eleven supermarkets in Managua (where almost a quarter of Nicaraguans live). To some extent the government fell into operating supermarkets. In the Somoza days these American-style supermarkets—one chain was appropriately named "Colonial"—catered to urban elites infatuated with U.S. lifestyles; they emphasize luxury and processed items. In the final days of the war the supermarkets were looted, leaving them bankrupt. ENABAS decided to finance their reopening, entering into a joint venture partnership with the original owners and often retaining the old managers. But these "Supermarkets of the People" are the same only at first glance: although located in the higher income neighborhoods, they now have poor customers from the barrios. The poor come to buy not the frozen vegetables (still available) but the basics at official prices: rice, corn, beans, sugar, salt, cooking oil, cheese.

To supply the same basic foods in the barrios at the official low prices, ENABAS created a new type of store, the *tienda popular* or people's store. By July 1982, 71 of these state-owned stores were in operation, theoretically selling 37 basic items in simple wood-plank buildings. Among the common complaints I've heard in the barrios is that the people's stores are only open during working hours (mom-and-pop stores stay open until late in the evening); that they don't give credit; and that they don't carry some of the things people want such as milk, chicken, vegetables, cheese, and fruits.

Supplementing these stores is a fleet of government-owned trucks ("mobile stores") which make the rounds every two weeks in many poor barrios and villages in Managua province. Each truck has the capacity to supply a thousand or so families with the basics.

The purpose of the stores and the mobile units is to cut out the middlemen and provide the basics at stable prices, especially for poor families. But a major shortcoming has been that they are still fundamentally middle-class in their design—they sell many items in larger packages than the truly poor can afford and they do not offer credit. On some of my first visits to barrios, I was surprised to find that poor people were paying higher than official prices even when a local ENABAS store or mobile unit was selling the same item at the official price. Then a Catholic nun living in a barrio explained to me that the *pulperías* (mom-and-pop stores) allow their customers to buy on credit, crucial for families with irregular employment. That's why government calls to denounce those who charge high prices often meet with little response, she said.

In addition, ENABAS supplies basic foodstuffs directly to commissaries set up in workplaces with over 30 workers. The administration of the workplace is required to supply space, and the trade union elects a committee to supervise the store. Since most such large workplaces are in Managua, so are most commissaries. By 1982, 500 were in operation in the capital. One apparently negative side effect concerns women. Since most of the shoppers are men—because the workers in these kinds of workplaces are mostly men—the women in their families sometimes feel marginalized since they "don't get to handle the money," according to comments I've heard.

ENABAS has also sought to develop a special "franchise" relationship with private retail stores with good reputations in their neighborhoods. The idea has been to take advantage of the honest storekeepers' managerial ability and wealth of knowledge about neighborhood needs and not to tax unnecessarily the limited capacities of ENABAS. The stores are called *expendios populares* or people's outlets. Over 1,000 of them were in operation by the end of 1981. In exchange for a pledge to sell controlled items at the official retail prices, a store owner is guaranteed an adequate supply of the items at official wholesale prices, thus ensuring a reasonable profit margin. The store owners must supply their own financing (although some government credit is available) and pick up their inventory from ENABAS warehouses. Storekeepers should gain extra benefit from their relationship with ENABAS because people patronizing the stores to buy basic items at the low official prices would undoubtedly buy other things too. In Managua, the largest volume of sales for ENABAS is through the *expendios populares*.

ENABAS is also making use of a traditional private distribution system—the large markets filled with stalls for private vendors. By building new markets in neighborhoods all over Managua, the government hopes to close down or at least reduce the sprawling Mercado Oriental (Eastern Market). This market, on the edge of the area leveled by the 1972 earthquake, has mushroomed to almost 10,000 vendors, mostly poor women. Because of its location, the Oriental requires long and costly trips for vendors and consumers alike. And it is known for hard-to-control price speculation (especially by a few large wholesalers), unsanitary conditions, and prostitution.

Thirty-six new neighborhood markets with stalls for private vendors have been built in Managua alone. For over a year they were highly promoted by newspaper ads featuring large maps of Managua and the caption, "Find your new market." Other ads, in photo-cartoon format, emphasize that new markets have high quality produce, are cleaner, better stocked, and provide lessons on hygiene and food preparation. And they also offer such amenities as barbershops.

The new market in the Ciudad Sandino barrio is an example of those the government would like to see flourish. Ciudad Sandino began as a settlement camp for families fleeing the 1970 flooding of Lake Managua; today it has 72,000 residents. In October 1981, Ciudad Sandino opened its own open air market, the pride of the barrio. The new market should save considerable time and bus money. In addition, it should promote the economy of the barrio, providing sources of employment which have been almost nonexistent in the past. One vendor in the new market, Fernando José Silva, explained to me why he was so enthusiastic. For five years he worked in the Oriental, paying 12 córdobas each day in bus fare; the new market is only two blocks from his home. Another vendor, Eva Maria Ulloa, told me how she used to have to board the bus at 5 in the morning to get to the Oriental by 7. Now she walks to work in a few minutes.

But the government has been largely frustrated in its desire to close down the Oriental. On my visit in June 1982 it seemed to be almost as large as ever, although perhaps better organized. People claim they continue to go there because they know they can find everything there, even though the prices for scarce products might be much higher than the official ones. They also claim that the beans are better there, the fish fresher, and the vegetables cheaper. In June I found vendors illegally but openly selling beans at 5.70 córdobas a pound, while "government" beans were going for the official 2.85 a pound. And because more people want to shop at the Oriental than at some of the comparatively immaculate new markets, vendors want to stay on at the Oriental. In the new markets some vendors claim they must charge higher prices because there are fewer customers. By mid-1982, government policymakers seemed to be backing away from their goal of closing down the Oriental, even though they still believed it would be in the people's best interests.

In rural areas, ENABAS has established over 200 rural supply centers which sell both basic foodstuffs and a few industrial goods at the official prices.

The Spoilers

As we have seen, shortages—often induced by rumors of scarcities and by hoarding by speculators—prompted the Sandinista-led government to fix price ceilings for basic necessities. Thus less than a year after victory its hopoes for an unregulated domestic food market had been abandoned. These same factors have made it far more difficult to enforce price ceilings than to set them. Sometimes, as we will see, the government has quite literally been left holding the bag.

Price gouging, even on items with official price ceilings, has been widespread in private outlets. Many retailers say they can't always sell at the official price because when an item is scarce, and ENABAS supplies are tied up in its own stores and the *expendios*, the wholesalers won't sell to them at the official wholesale prices.

Many vendors dodge the rules by selling a scarce product, such as cooking oil, at the official price—but only if the customer agrees to buy something else (that she or he might not even want) at a higher price. Another tactic is to sell at the official prices when a nearby people's store or *expendio* is well supplied. But as soon as the rice or cooking oil or beans or soap runs out in the government-supplied outlet, then the private seller jacks up the price. A secret government survey in August 1981 showed that 93 out of 100 stalls in the Oriental were selling scarce basic food items above the official prices.

The government has been reluctant to use police methods to keep down prices. In addition, paying inspectors is expensive, and in mid-1981 there were only 40 for the entire country. Nonetheless, in the first six months of 1981, 625 wholesale and retail vendors were fined a total of 230,000 córdobas.

The Sugar Blues

Sugar is one product which illustrates the government's headaches in enforcing price ceilings. (While you might think people would be better off with less sugar, most Nicaraguans don't see it that way.) The trouble started in 1980 when the government underestimated the portion of the sugar harvest needed for the domestic market and thus "oversold" it— mainly to the Coca-Cola Company. Demand was growing for sugar, as for other food items, precisely because of the improved purchasing power of the rural and urban poor. One of the most successfully reactivated industries has been the bottled soft drink industry—the revolution tripled Coke and Pepsi sales in 1980, compared to 1978.

By April 1980, rumors of a coming scarcity of sugar set off an explosion in purchases. One rumor had it that Nicaragua's sugar had been sent off to communist Cuba—a Caribbean version of coals to Newcastle. Some who had the means began storing sugar for the future. Others began hoarding in order to speculate. Monthly sales of sugar soared to the equivalent of 12 pounds per person. Such increased sales, of course, guaranteed that there actually would be a shortage. Government supermarkets became easy targets; whole families would swoop down and buy up ten five-pound sacks. Speculators paid poor families to go into supermarkets several times, buying over 100 pounds of sugar a day to be sold at much higher prices in the Eastern Market.

The government first responded by using every communication medium to tell people that there would be enough sugar for everyone if no one hoarded, and that the country desperately needed the foreign exchange it could earn from sugar exports. Posters went up everywhere: "A good revolutionary consumes less sugar daily." I found the slogan convenient when explaining to startled juice vendors that, no, I really would rather not have a few tablespoons of sugar added to my glass of fresh orange juice, a common Nicaraguan practice.

A blitz of television and radio spots told how sugar can be bad for you. Dr. So-and-so, head of the school of dentistry of the national university, looked up from a patient's mouth into the camera: "We know that people who consume sugar are more likely to develop cavities." Fade to announcer: "Reduce your sugar consumption and help rebuild the economy of the nation. Each spoonful of sugar that we save permits Nicaragua to export more and thus obtain foreign currency to satisfy our needs and develop the country. When we consume sugar rationally, we are saving. Each teaspoon that we save is converted into foreign currency."

These sugar-is-bad-for-you spots probably did not have the desired effect. In my experience, most people were skeptical about such messages; they suspected the real reason they were being told something wasn't good for them was that the government couldn't deliver the item in question. Perhaps more effective was an incentive program. If a muncipality reduced its per capita sugar intake, thereby allowing the country to export more, part of the dollar value earned was returned to the municipality in córdobas for financing local public works. The government calculated that this incentive program saved over $500,000 worth of sugar in only eight months.

Yet another installment in the government's sugar blues

came in late 1981. First were several production problems: heavy rains in May reduced the expected crop yields by 12 percent. Then work stoppages, organized by antigovernment communist unions in the sugar mills, cost 700 tons a day. Finally, the Mexican government ran into its own big sugar shortage and pressured the Nicaraguan government to sell it 17,000 tons of refined sugar. Since Mexico was helping the new government diplomatically and financially (including supplies of oil on long-term credit), the Nicaraguan government felt that it could not turn Mexico down. (However, I imagine there were many officials who were highly annoyed by the Mexican "request.")

Nicaragua was left with short supplies. What refined sugar was available the government decided to sell to small candymakers and bakers since raw sugar would be "unacceptable" to them. Left for sale on the retail market was only raw sugar, which normally would be exported. Raw sugar became the cause célèbre of the day. Antigovernment forces spread rumors that the beloved white sugar had disappeared from Nicaragua forever. Once again, rumors set off an all-out scramble—corruption, pilfering, black markets, etc.—to corner the scarce refined sugar. Progovernment papers churned out numerous articles explaining why white sugar wasn't available and that brown sugar is really better for you anyway. (A favorite headline of mine in El Nuevo Diario heralded the "Great Vitamin Properties of Raw Sugar." The article went on for paragraphs in a highly scientific tenor, citing experiments with monkeys who ate only raw sugar and didn't develop tooth decay. It made raw sugar sound like the greatest health food of all time.)

Several other basic foodstuffs illustrate the same story: government programs to make food available at stable, affordable prices undercut by profiteering as well as by those holding food in "reserve," for fear of shortages. Thus part of the national economic emergency declared on September 9, 1981 made it a crime to hoard, speculate, or disseminate false information that might provoke hoarding and speculation. In addition, in a major break with private marketing, the emergency decree placed exclusive authority for domestic sugar sales into the government's hands.

"Guaranty Cards"—*Not* Rationing

In early 1982, ENABAS introduced a system of "guaranty cards," thus sidestepping the dreaded word "rationing." The system had first been tried in a Managua barrio, apparently after the CDS neighborhood organizations pushed for it. When the government first introduced the cards in March, those against the revolution thought they had been handed a golden opportunity to discredit the government—"See, it's just going to be another Cuba!" But the cards, combined with putting sugar sales exclusively in government-supplied outlets, did stabilize the price at the official ceiling by making it possible for all families to buy about five pounds of sugar per person per month. (In the Eastern Market, some illegal sales of sugar—at much higher prices—persisted, but there was no crackdown, apparently in order to allow an escape valve for those who simply "had" to have than five pounds of sugar a month.)

The CDSs, the Sandinista neighborhood organizations, were actively involved in organizing the sugar distribution system. They carried out a household census and issued the guaranty cards. (Several Nicaraguans tell about their experiences with sugar distribution in our companion book, *Now We Can Speak*.) By June, only three months later, the whole card system was so widely accepted that the maligners of the government were quiet, and I found government officials taking satisfaction in a small but politically important triumph. While the government had found it necessary to eliminate sugar sales through the private market, at least the government's sugar blues were over.

The Question of Subsidies

Government subsidies on food staples have been fundamental to whatever gains have been made in the food security of the poor majority. To counteract the effects of persistent unemployment and overall inflation, ENABAS has been wholesaling and retailing food for a lot less than it pays to buy it from farmers or import it. In 1982–83, for example, ENABAS is buying beans from campesinos at 3.50 córdobas a pound and retailing them at 2.85 a pound, plus absorbing all the costs of transport, drying, storing, packaging, administration, etc. With many millions of pounds, it adds up to a staggering cost.

Paying higher prices to help motivate producers further increases the subsidies. In fact, the government projected total ENABAS subsidies to come to a staggering one billion córdobas in 1982. Not only is this subsidy enormous, but is not targeted to the poor. If anything, the poorest are discriminated against by programs that market low-priced foods through workplaces, since the really poor don't have permanent workplaces—that's their basic problem! By 1981, however, ENABAS started to eliminate people's stores and *expendios* from better-off neighborhoods in order to concentrate more in poorer neighborhoods.

A major threat to the well-being of those who need the food subsidies is that increasingly severe foreign exchange shortages will pressure the government to severely cut back or do away with the subsidy program. In Spring 1982 the government placed large display advertisements in the newspapers to promote public awareness of the magnitude of the food subsidies, emphasizing that such outlays require sacrificing other programs.

Comparing the prices of staple foods in Nicaragua with prices elsewhere in Central America shows the results of applying the "logic of the majority" to food policies in Nicaragua. Beans sold for 2.87 córdobas a pound in Nicaragua, 4.60 in Guatemala, 4.80 in El Salvador and Honduras, and 7.50 in Costa Rica, according to an August 1982 *Barricada* survey. Rice sold for 2.94 córdobas a pound in Nicaragua, 3.30 in Guatemala, 4.00 in El Salvador, 4.80 in Honduras and 7.00 in Costa Rica. (Prices were converted into córdobas at the official exchange rate.)

While their subsidized prices are already generally higher than Nicaragua's, Nicaragua's neighbors are being pressured by the International Monetary Fund to abolish consumer food subsidies. Following suit would be politically very damaging to the popular base of the revolution, and it is highly unlikely the Sandinistas would do so. But indiscriminate subsidies are incompatible with urgent fiscal austerity and, as the government itself points out, severely limit other programs of benefit to the poor majority. Thus the real challenge facing the

Sandinistas on the third anniversary of victory was to develop discriminatory subsidies—subsidies that discriminate
in favor of the poor majority, placing the burden on those
who can afford it. *That* would be revolutionary.

Are People Eating Better Now?

It's hard to document whether people are eating better now.
We know that overall food consumption is up about 40 percent since before the war. Undoubtedly it is not the rich and
the upper middle-class minority that is eating more, for they
have never gone without. But the other Nicaraguans—the
majority—cannot be lumped together when we try to assess
their food well-being.

In the countryside, those with access to land—households
making up perhaps 40 percent of Nicaragua's population—
are now using more of what they produce, both directly
and through consumption of small livestock, most observers
agree. As the revolution lowers rents, abolishes sharecropping, and gives land or better quality land to the land-poor
and landless, these campesino families will likely be eating
better and have real food security for the first time in their
lives. Asked how they're eating now, compared to before,
many campesinos tell me, "We're getting by okay." And they
proudly point out the many chickens and pigs running loose
around their peasant homes.

Life is tougher for the majority in the city as well as for
rural laborers without land. And prospects are threatening.
A survey of Managua in early 1982 yielded no evidence of
overall improvement in the diet of the poor majority. Ma-
naguans, without land to grow food and hardest hit by inflation, were eating more of less expensive foods. Rice, bean,
and sugar consumption had gone up while milk and red meat
consumption had dropped.

Such a survey, however, must be taken at best as an ap-
proximation of trends rather than as hard data. Also useful
are the firsthand observations of those who have lived for
years in the poorer barrios. In June 1981 I asked several
Catholic Sisters if the people were eating better now. "The
children now look healthier, even chubby," one Sister responded, with others agreeing. This Sister is a nurse, aware

of the signs of even first-degree malnutrition which, according to a 1975 U.S. A.I.D. study, afflicted 42 percent of Nicaraguan children under four. She and other medical workers agree that infant deaths are many fewer than before, even though births are undoubtedly on the rise (apparently the usual postwar phenomenon). While improved family nutrition is a likely factor in this important advance for the poor majority, other causes could be even more important, including newly created neighborhood infant rehydration stations for babies suffering from diarrhea, a campaign to encourage breastfeeding and neighborhood sanitation efforts.

Steady employment is crucial in determining how well people eat. Families with at least one or two members regularly employed, no matter the wages, obviously fare better than those whose members live catch-as-catch-can. In the first two years, the government did greatly increase the number of jobs, mainly in the government sector. With a deepening fiscal crisis in mid-1981, the government started to make across-the-board hiring cutbacks. The overall economic picture for 1982 is bleaker yet—and what is most frustrating for the Sandinistas is that so many crucial factors are outside Nicaragua's control, notably the steep slide in international prices for Nicaragua's chief exports. As in the rest of Central America, foreign exchange is growing very scarce. That spells disaster for the country's manufacturing sector, which is dependent on imported inputs as well as sales of its manufactures to the other countries in the region, facing their own financial crises. Large-scale factory shutdowns are likely, increasing unemployment. Growing inflation, still less than half that in neighboring Costa Rica in 1981, will chop away at the purchasing power even of those with jobs. While the real purchasing power of urban workers has dropped since 1978, government measures to control basic food prices have undoubtedly helped at least maintain the majority's food consumption. Government price controls are more likely to have been effective in neighborhoods with a greater degree of self-organization, where there is willingness to stand up to price gougers. Thus an important part of the majority's food security depends on large numbers of people organizing themselves on their own behalf. Overall food prices since mid-1981 have risen more slowly than prices of other goods, especially those imported or made from imported materials. This is due to the general impact of the price ceilings on basic foods, controls (and built-in government subsidies), and the fact that food is mostly not imported. This is particularly the case since late 1981, when the growing scarcity of foreign ex-change led the government to significantly hike taxes on im-ported consumer goods. As a result, lower income people are more likely to find items like shoes and radios out of reach, but food a relatively good buy.

The Last Straw

Ten days of better-build-an-ark rains (21 inches in one day alone!) struck Nicaragua's Pacific coast in late May 1982. According to a United Nations survey, rain and flooding swept away at least 20,000 acres of just-planted food crops, $3.6 million in stored grains, and innumerable rural roads, and did $350 million additional damage to the nation's eco-nomic infrastructure. This was a tremendous loss in a coun-try where all goods and services produced in an entire year (GDP) are worth only $2.2 billion.

Arriving the day after the rains, I found a country out-raged at the opportunistic hoarding and speculation by pri-vate merchants, especially wholesalers. Public sentiment was so strong that it was easy for the government to move quickly and decisively. The day after I arrived the national police were authorized to inspect food prices and arrest speculators. Fines were increased and jail sentences of up to six months were imposed. In the first two days alone, the media were filled with stories of the arrest of two big wholesalers and 111 retailers. One retailer showed receipts proving that he had paid so much to the wholesaler that he had to raise his price; his fine was dropped and his goods returned to him, while a stiff fine was slapped on the wholesaler.

Labor unions, the CDS neighborhood organizations, the national women's organization, and a lot of ordinary people were calling for a guaranty card system for beans, rice, and corn "since it has worked so well with sugar." At this writing (September 1982) a new law to do so is being intensely de-bated while ENABAS is rapidly expanding the number of franchised private retail stores (*expendios*) and, where necessary, opening people's stores.

Three years' experience has raised deep doubts whether the free market can serve the poor majority, at least in times of scarcity. It has also shown how difficult it is for a new government to set up an efficient, low cost alternative system.

FOURTEEN

REFLECTIONS

FOR OVER THREE YEARS WE HAVE WATCHED the Nicaraguan people struggle to build a just, productive food and farming system. And this struggle is paying off. Despite the enormous legacy of underdevelopment and the powerful forces determined to derail the Nicaraguan economy, the postwar reactivation of agricultural production has been extraordinarily rapid. More acres have been planted and yields have been improved in most major products, both food crops for local consumption as well as export crops. More than 45,000 landless workers have gotten access to lands where they can grow food for their own consumption. And the base is being laid for a food system operating in the interests of the poor majority.

But what has impressed us most—even more than the material advances—is the way that the Nicaraguans have pursued their fundamental goal: to reorient their entire economy to serve the needs of the majority. We are struck by their seriousness of purpose, by their reasonableness and perseverance in the face of gross misrepresentations of their policies and unremitting threats against them. We have been impressed also by their adaptive pragmatism. But perhaps most of all we have been impressed by their unyielding faith in themselves. Faced with staggering odds, they have maintained their faith in the capacity of human beings to create history according to their ideals of justice, compassion, and rational planning.

We have seen that the Sandinista approach to agrarian reform is not vindictive. It does not penalize the rich simply for being wealthy. But in contrast to the privileged place of wealth under the Somoza regime, it makes clear that the possession of needed productive resources carries with it an obligation to produce. If that obligation is not met, then the government has the responsibility to put those resources into the hands of those who will use them productively.

Neither is the Sandinista approach to agrarian and food reform oppressively idealistic. It does not assume that the individual's self-interest must, on principle, be quashed in order to serve the community. The urgent question for the Sandinista leaders is not how to stifle individual self-interest but how to build economic structures in which people do not have to choose between themselves and community needs, in which people can serve both simultaneously.

From the start the Sandinistas have been wary of government takeover of economic activity. "Profit" has not been, for them, an inherently dirty word. Indeed they have gone far beyond what their left critics would allow in seeking to provide incentives that would motivate capitalist farmers to renew export production, peasant farmers to increase the nation's supply of food, and food merchants to efficiently market it.

The Sandinista approach to reform is participatory. New policies have usually been developed in active cooperation with those most directly affected. Indeed, we have seen how one draft of the agrarian reform law was scrapped when the organization of rural workers complained that they had not been adequately consulted. The Sandinistas assume that people can only effectively participate if those with common interests are organized to promote their interests. Thus the government has encouraged the development of special interest organizations—of small farmers and ranchers, farm laborers, youth, and women—while working with the previously established associations of the elite agricultural producers.

A participatory approach to development assumes a voluntary approach. The government has not, for example, forced rural people to join cooperatives, even though the Sandinistas believe that, for many, cooperatives offer a chance for much more rapid economic and social advancement.

Of course, the Sandinistas have made mistakes. And there is much to criticize. Both in this book and in its companion volume, *Now We Can Speak: A Journey Through the New Nicaragua*, we discuss numerous specific mistakes; Nicaraguan leaders themselves are self-critical about many of them. But here in our "reflections," we are attempting to cull our essential impressions of the leadership's underlying values. In regard to farming and food policies, we have concluded that the Nicaraguans' mistakes have been honest mistakes, rooted primarily in inexperience, overwork, and lack of adequate information.

One could in fact make a very strong case that the Sandinistas gravest error has been an overemphasis on trying to keep all social classes happy—what they call a policy of "national unity." Among other things, this has meant continuing to import many luxuries—from teething rings to Chivas Regal—which only the well-off can buy. Yet the hard work and sacrifices needed to pay off the mounting foreign debt aggravated by this policy will ultimately fall most heavily on the poorer classes.

The first three years of the Nicaraguan revolution have required the Sandinistas to address dilemmas without painless solutions:

—How can Nicaragua satisfy the basic needs of the majority—rather than the profit "needs" of the minority— while maintaining a mixed economy with most production in private hands?

—How can Nicaragua maintain political pluralism and at the same time make the profound structural changes demanded by the majority, whose expectations have been rising since the overthrow of the Somoza dictatorship's system of economic and political exploitation? How can Nicaragua increase the political power of those who have been powerless without creating a counter-revolutionary reaction from the wealthy who are accustomed to wielding political power far in excess of their numbers?

—How can the new Nicaragua live as a sovereign, independent nation, treated with respect by the United States, when Nicaragua is located in its strategic "back yard"?

—How can Nicaragua create this new relationship during a new Cold War between the U.S. and the U.S.S.R., with the most reactionary president in decades occupying the White House?

—How can Nicaragua make revolutionary internal transformations literally in the middle of a Central America undergoing the greatest political and economic crisis in its history?

The Sandinistas have had to choose answers and solutions to these dilemmas, even when they were obviously far from ideal. But both the Reagan administration and the Sandinistas' Nicaraguan opponents have chosen to ignore these critical dilemmas. Instead they have busied themselves with criticisms of the Sandinistas' difficult answers to these difficult questions. None of the Sandinistas' critics have cared enough to offer any alternative answers.

Most Americans know little of such agonizing choices. All they hear from the U.S. government and press are charges against Nicaragua for infringements of freedom of the press, relocation of the Miskito Indians, or imprisonment of National Guardsmen. We do not dismiss such charges out of hand, excusing the government by balancing their failures against their socially responsible policies. Instead, we try to find out the truth behind such charges, interviewing both Nicaraguans and North Americans living in the country. What we have learned is not that the Nicaraguan government is blameless but that the reality is a far cry from the alleged "totalitarianism" decried by the Reagan administration and echoed by much of the U.S. press. We ask ourselves to what degree some of these actions by the Nicaraguan government, such as limitations on freedom of the press, are a defensive reaction to threats from the United States. For when a government feels attacked from the outside, attacks from the inside seem even more threatening.

Internal Opposition

An observer from afar might assume that since Somoza and his closest associates fled after his defeat, internal opposition would be minimal. But in Nicaragua the propertied classes did not exit en masse as they have in the wake of some other revolutionary victories. Many stayed, assuming that the government would still be in their hands. In fact, with Somoza out of their way, many expected to do even better financially—and many have.

What has made the elite so angry, we were told by many Nicaraguans, is not that the new government has taken their wealth. It hasn't. What enrages so many of the wealthy is that they have lost their power to determine the nation's priorities. While the majority of industry and agricultural production remains in private hands, the important decisions are being made in the interests of the poor majority, not in the interests of the big business associations such as COSEP.

While some capitalists, including some of the nation's wealthiest, are producing and investing (the Sandinista leadership calls them the "patriotic capitalists"), the majority have not only refused to invest but have been sending their assets out of the country. "Decapitalization"—meaning everything from letting your farm and equipment run down to sending your money to a Miami bank—has thus become a household word to even the barely literate Nicaraguan. During the first three years, decapitalization has seriously damaged the country's efforts to rebuild.

Under Somoza over 80 percent of investment came from the private sector; by 1981, only 10 percent. Half a billion dollars illegally left the country between mid-1980 and mid-1981. Thus the majority of investment has to be drawn from the impoverished public sector.

The propertied classes have had another, perhaps even more powerful weapon to use against a government whose priorities they can no longer determine: their influence over public opinion.

Under Somoza, the newspaper *La Prensa* became a national symbol of resistance. In 1978, its respected editor Pedro Joaquin Chamorro was killed by the National Guard. After the Sandinista victory, a dogmatically anti-Sandinista son of Pedro Joaquin, who had never worked on the paper, took over *La Prensa*. In protest, Pedro Joaquin's brother, who had worked closely with him, and 80 percent of the staff walked out and founded an independent paper sympathetic to the revolution, *El Nuevo Diario*. Another son of Pedro Joaquin became head of the daily newspaper of the Sandinista Front, *Barricada*.

La Prensa, however, remains the most influential of the three. Its history as the "principled opposition" to the dictator, its strong financial backing (including help from foreign donors), its superior production and distribution system, as well as its sensationalist approach to news, bring *La Prensa* as many readers as the other two papers combined.

While the U.S. press still portrays *La Prensa* as the principled opposition, actually reading the paper—as I often have—gives a different impression. In fact, *La Prensa* blends rumors, virulent attacks on the government, hysterical anti-communism, and biased treatment of news stories—all in a campaign to undermine the government's programs. And more might be at work than meets the eye; documented research on the CIA's influence in major newspapers in Allende's Chile and Manley's Jamaica points to very striking similarities with *La Prensa*. (See Fred Landis' article, listed in our Bibliography.)

The Sandinista government has been roundly criticized for briefly closing down *La Prensa* from time to time for printing stories which the government charges are libelous or damaging to the country's precarious economy. Nevertheless, in visiting Nicaragua, one cannot help but be struck by the intense debate carried out almost daily by the country's three newspapers. The intense exchange hardly fits with the "totalitarian" image our government paints of Nicaragua. And neither do many other aspects of life in Nicaragua today, as we discuss below.

Close to Uncle Sam

To understand this book, you must place the new farm and food programs in the context of the Nicaragua of today, understanding the obstacles with which the new leadership—and all Nicaraguans—must grapple. The most powerful single obstacle facing Nicaragua today is the unrelenting hostility of the United States government.

Unable to prevent the Sandinista-led overthrow of the Somoza dictatorship despite last-minute maneuverings, the Carter administration sought to work out a *modus vivendi* with the new Nicaraugan government. But the Reagan administration came in slinging. Its belligerence encouraged Nicaragua's elite to drain their wealth from the country.

While supporting governments in neighboring El Salvador and Guatemala notorious for their indiscriminate slaughter of civilians, the Reagan administration singled out Nicaragua as a target for outlandish allegation, verbal and military threats, international isolation and a $19 million CIA covert operation.

Labeling Nicaragua a "Marxist-Leninist" state, the Reagan administration chooses to ignore the fact that most of the internal economy—80 percent in the case of agriculture —remains in private hands after three years of revolution.

Claiming Nicaragua is a major human rights violator, the Reagan administration accuses the new Nicaraguan government of being "more repressive" than the Somoza dictatorship, contrary to reports by a variety of human rights organizations. Amnesty International, Americas Watch, and Pax Christi International, as well as the human rights division of the Organization of American States, have each concluded that there's a world of difference for the better between Nicaragua today and Nicaragua under the Somoza dictatorship. (Nicaragua stands out as the only Latin American country ever to have *invited* the Organization of American States to investigate its human rights policy—including the situation of indigenous people.)

The Reagan administration also chooses to ignore the fact that the Sandinistas did not summarily execute the National Guardsmen but, after individual trials, let half go free. And it ignores the transformation of a country previously characterized by torture and summary executions into one where government-sanctioned torture and even capital punishment have been abolished.

Charging that Nicaragua has become "totalitarian," the Reagan administration chooses to ignore the considerable freedom—of speech, of religion, of association, and of the press—certainly compared to most other Latin American countries. Several opposition political parties and trade unions, on both the right and left, are small but vigorous. The Catholic Church, increasingly divided in its response to the Sandinista revolution, continues as a major cultural and political force. Protestant churches, including a multitude of new right-wing fundamentalist sects, flourish. In the markets, bars, buses and streets one hears plenty of complaints, criticisms and downright attacks (as you'll hear in our companion volume, *Now We Can Speak: A Journey Through the New Nicaragua*).

The Reagan administration could have chosen to encourage the positive steps—in justice for the poor as well as in civil liberties—taken by the new government. Instead it has chosen only to exaggerate to the point of distortion the revolution's shortcomings.

And on the basis of these distortions, the United States continues unabated its campaign of threat and intervention against Nicaragua:

—In 1981 the U.S. abruptly cut off vitally needed wheat loans to Nicaragua on the pretext that the Nicaraguans were supplying arms to the Salvadoran guerillas. The same day as the cut-off, however, the State Department itself claimed that "Nicaragua had virtually halted all flow of arms."

—The State Department has repeatedly announced contingency plans for an invasion of Nicaragua. In October 1981, joint U.S.-Honduran naval maneuvers simulated a naval blockade of the country and U.S. warships have been stationed off the Nicaraguan coast. In addition, the U.S. is spending $21 million to expand three Honduran airstrips so they can handle U.S. transport planes and fighters.

—In February 1982, the *Washington Post* revealed that the administration had approved a $19 million plan to create a Latin American paramilitary force to blow up bridges and power stations in Nicaragua. (Such sabotage was subsequently carried out.) Under the plan, the U.S. is providing training, money, and weapons to former National Guardsmen in Honduras, as well as encouraging agitation against the Nicaraguan government among some of the Miskito Indians.

—The U.S. has tripled aid to the Honduran military, which collaborates with the ex-members of Somoza's National Guard staging incursions into Nicaragua from encampments in Honduras. In August 1982, U.S. troops from Panama helped the Honduran army set up a base—including an airstrip for jet fighters—just 25 miles from the Nicaraguan border.

—In early 1982, the U.S. blocked a $30 million loan from the Inter-American Development Bank that would have revitalized Nicaragua's fishing industry; opposed a $16 million World Bank loan to Nicaragua for city development projects; and blocked a $5 million U.N. Development Program grant for a survey of rural people's basic needs.

—The U.S. government pressures allied governments around the world not to give economic aid to Nicaragua. It succeeded in pressuring Canada to choose Honduras instead of Nicaragua as the country on which to concentrate its economic aid in the region, despite a Parliamentary Commission's highly favorable fact-finding tour of Nicaragua.

—In defiance of U.S. law, the administration continues to turn a blind eye to paramilitary camps in Florida where anti-Sandinista forces train for armed intervention.

—Despite repeated efforts by the Nicaraguan government to seek an accomodation with the United States, the Reagan administration has refused to enter into talks.

In March 1982, the Nicaraguan government declared a 30-day State of National Emergency, giving it authority to limit rights because of the threats of military intervention. This decision came soon after the Reagan administration's approval of a covert "destabilization" campaign was leaked to the press, heightened attacks from ex-National Guard forces encamped in Honduras, the blowing up of two major highway bridges and a thwarted plot to destroy the country's only cement factory and oil refinery. The State of National Emergency did not establish a curfew or martial law, nor has it blocked the progress of government programs such as the agrarian reform. Continued threats have led the government to periodically renew the State of National Emergency.

The view from the United States

Here in the United States, our government is moving in precisely the opposite direction from that which the Nicaraguan revolution has committed itself. In favor here are economic policies callously penalizing the poor while further enriching the wealthy minority.

Our government justifies its anti-majority policies on the grounds that only austerity for poor and middle income people can foster a resurgence of American "free enterprise," the guarantor of progress and protector of our liberties. Our government, our business leaders, our media stress that the only alternative is authoritarian socialism, with its inefficiency and denial of human liberties. Awakening to the limitations of the American system, yet presented with only this alternative, no wonder many Americans are bereft of hope altogether.

By focusing only on Nicaragua's shortcomings—and seriously distorting them—our government and mass media rob us Americans of the opportunity to learn from people who believe differently, who believe that something new is possible.

So at a time when the world's people are desperately in need of "good news," I have felt privileged. Not in being able to latch on to a new development model but by being allowed to witness the courage of a poor, small country to experiment, to be original, to think for itself, to not slavishly follow models.

But, the U.S. government tells us, we all should be frightened of this tiny country to our south. According to Washington, Nicaragua is an beachhead of Soviet influence. The Reagan administration refuses to rule out armed intervention against Nicaragua. It shamelessly admits clandestine maneuvers to topple the government. It arms Nicaragua's enemies. And it does not hesitate a moment to make false accusations against the Nicaraguan government.

As Americans, we are saddened to admit that we can only describe U.S. policy toward Nicaragua immoral. It is immoral because it can do nothing but harm all Nicaraguans.

An attempt to actually overthrow the Sandinista government would result in unspeakable bloodshed. Any outside intervention would be overwhelmingly interpreted by Nicaraguans as an attempt to deny them what they have earned by their suffering. Hundreds of thousands of Nicaraguans have already endured grave personal sacrifices, as the many tombstones, plaques and monuments to fallen martyrs of the war testify. Having sacrificed their loved ones to assert their right to self-determination, they would not let go of it easily.

Virtually no one within Nicaragua supports U.S. policy. Even the harshest critics of the Sandinistas realize that Washington's policies can only contribute to a shrinking of the space for critical voices, to the kind of national fear that leads neighbors to suspect neighbors. Given our government's treatment of Japanese-American citizens during World War II, surely we should be aware of this danger. A U.S.-provoked war, by direct intervention or by proxy, would most endanger the very opposition figures that U.S. policy supposedly supports, as even *La Prensa* has publicly recognized.

Nicaraguans of every social class have told us again and again: "Leave us alone to find our own way, to make our own mistakes, to determine our own history for the first time since the beginning of colonialism."

As we finish this book in September 1982, we hope it is not too late. We hope that the U.S. government has not already gone so far in its threats and aggressions as to insure the destruction of what is genuinely creative and democratic about the Nicaraguan "school." For if the United States succeeds in its goal, it is not just the people of Nicaragua who will lose.

The U.S. government must realize that Nicaragua poses no military or economic threat. The threat it could pose is the threat of a good example—an example to the poor majorities elsewhere in Central America and around the third world who still suffer tyranny similar to that which the Nicaraguans endured under Somoza.

What if the Sandinistas help to teach us all that there could be more than two models of development—that it *is* possible to combine grassroots participation with profound structural change? From El Salvador, to the Philippines, to Poland the answer is desperately awaited. Surely our government must know that if the Nicaraguan revolution did succeed in meeting its people's basic needs while creating a genuine democracy, then our government's fight against revolutionary movements of the poor and hungry throughout the world would be that much more difficult.

Could our government fear that unless it can force the Sandinista revolution to become "another Cuba"—"proving" the White House was right all along—then it will be more difficult to mobilize the public opinion, the tax dollars and the American youths necessary to fight against the uprisings of the hungry and dispossessed around the world?

If these are the real fears motivating U.S. government policies toward Nicaragua, there is another, more sobering lesson for Americans: It may be that we will never know whether the vision the Sandinistas are attempting is possible as long as we maintain in power in Washington those intent on denying it even a chance.

EDUCATION AND OTHER SOCIAL INDICATORS

	1978	1982
Illiteracy Rate	50.35	12.07
Education Expenditure —thousands of cordobas	341,024	1,159,876
Percentage of GNP for Education	1.32	4.25 (1981)
Total Students	501,660	1,000,103
Adult Education Students	none	242,587
Infant Mortality	121	94
	1000 births	1000 (1981)
Vaccinations	810,000	1,740,000
Health Budget (cordobas)	373,000	1,231,000 (1981)

Source: *Envio* 13, Instituto Historico Centroamericano, Managua, July 1982. *Programa Bienestar Social* (health expenditures).

DISTRIBUTION OF LANDHOLDINGS BY SIZE (1971)

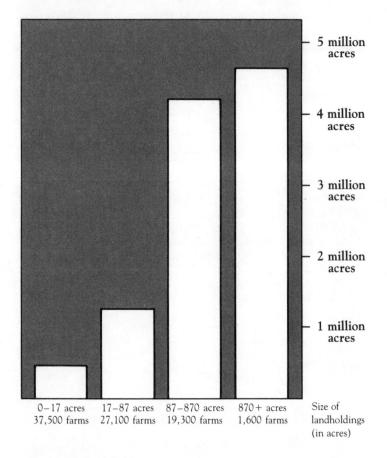

				— 5 million acres
				— 4 million acres
				— 3 million acres
				— 2 million acres
				— 1 million acres

0–17 acres	17–87 acres	87–870 acres	870+ acres	Size of landholdings
37,500 farms	27,100 farms	19,300 farms	1,600 farms	(in acres)

Note: Acreage represents amount of land owned, not amount of land planted.

Source: Fondo Internacional de Desarrollo Agricola, *Informe de la Mision Especial de Programacion a Nicaragua*, 1981, p. 39.

AGRICULTURAL POPULATION OF NICARAGUA (1978)

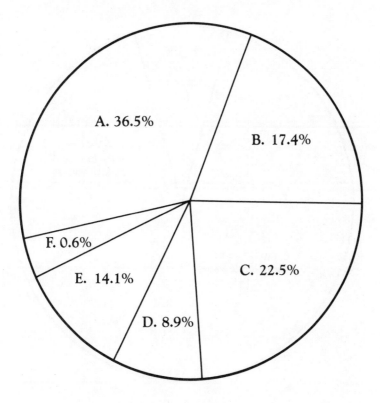

A. Holders of less than subsistence parcels
B. Seasonal farm laborers
C. Holders of subsistence parcels
D. Holders of medium-size parcels
E. Fulltime salaried workers
F. Owners and managers of large landholdings

Source: CIERA

DISTRIBUTION OF RURAL INCOME (1972)

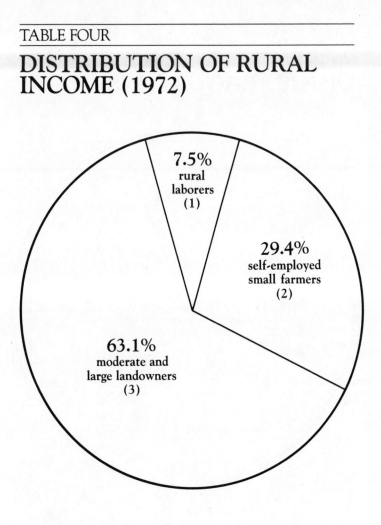

7.5%
rural
laborers
(1)

29.4%
self-employed
small farmers
(2)

63.1%
moderate and
large landowners
(3)

(1) 51% of economically active rural population
(2) 45.5% of economically active rural population
(3) 3.5% of economically active rural population

Source: *Unidad de Analisis Sectorial*, FAO Informe, 1979

NUTRITIONAL INTAKE BY INCOME GROUP (1971)

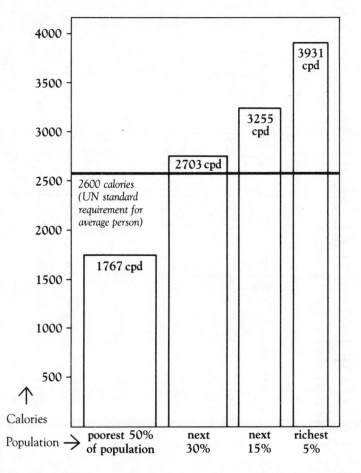

Note: The richest 5 percent of the population consumed 2.2 times more calories than the poorest 50 percent; 2.5 times more protein; and 3.5 times more fats.

Source: Fondo Internacional de Desarrollo Agricola, *Informe de la Mision Especial de Programacion a Nicaragua*, 1981, p. 54

PRODUCTION OF PRINCIPAL AGRICULTURAL CROPS, 1977–78 THROUGH 1982–83

Index, 1977–78 = 100

	48–52[1]	61–65[1]	1970[2]	77–78	79–80[4]	80–81[4]	81–82[4]	82–83[4] (projections)
Export Products								
Raw Cotton	6.5	60.7	55.0	100	17.7	61.6	53.2	68.7
Sesame	216.8	108.5	145.9	100	90.4	161.0	128.2	173.6
Bananas	11.2	193.1	187.1	100	94.5	93.8	103.6	117.1
Coffee	31.5	50.4	67.7	100	98.2	102.7	109.5	113.5
Cane Sugar	22.3	39.1	62.7	100	86.5	97.8	118.7	130.6
Tobacco (havana)	21.6[3]	26.7[3]	79.5[3]	100	128.9	107.5	97.0	143.0
Domestic Products								
Rice	45.5	111.8	225.7	100	132.1	130.3	188.8	225.3
Beans	46.1	102.0	127.8	100	71.0	69.8	145.4	159.3
Corn	57.9	94.3	124.1	100	80.4	101.4	110.5	142.3
Sorghum	84.2	107.5	145.7	100	148.3	208.5	209.8	246.9

1. multi-year average   2. calendar year   3. includes rubio and havana   4. one crop cycle

Source: FAO yearbooks, 1948–52 to 1970; Information and Analysis Branch, Office of Agricultural Production, Export and Livestock (based on 1980 Statistical Yearbook of Nicaragua (INEC), P.A.N. and the 1982–83 Plan for the Agricultural Sector (MIDINRA)) for 1977–78 to 1982–83.

CROP ACREAGE IN NICARAGUA FOR MAJOR CROPS, 1948–1982

Crop	1948–52[1]	1967	1974–76[1]	% increase 48–52 to 74–76[3]	1981–82[4]
Cotton	51,870	363,090	427,310	+823%	231,285
Coffee	138,320	200,514[2]	207,480	+150%	259,906
Sugarcane	37,050	61,750	98,800	+266%	109,749
Rice	44,460	64,220	69,160	+155%	103,474
Sesame	51,870	24,700	19,760	−262%	35,711
Corn	251,940	563,160	573,140	+227%	497,863
Beans	64,220	163,020	155,610	+242%	221,582
Sorghum	81,510	130,910	140,790	+172%	138,140
TOTAL	721,240		1,692,050	+234	1,597,710

1. multi-year average
2. average for 1961–65
3. population increase in this period was approximately 213%
4. one crop cycle

Source: Fondo Internacional de Desarrollo Agrícola (FIDA), columns 1 and 3; FAO, column 3; *Tres Anos de Reforma Agraria*, Ministerio de Desarrollo Agropecuario y Reforma Agraria, Government of Nicaragua.

TABLE EIGHT

EXPORT OF MAJOR AGRICULTURAL COMMODITIES
(IN THOUSANDS OF TONS)

	1948–52	1956	1969	1972	1978	1979	1980	1981[1]
Sugar	6.30	4.38	62.89	81.28	104.92	89.36	67.91	85.60
Coffee	15.75	17.17	30.37	32.72	51.34	54.52	46.12	49.17
Cotton	3.55	36.88	68.84	116.84	131.70	111.80	19.52[2]	72.00
Bananas	13.00	4.37	22.35	42.67	136.14	117.29	103.34	150.26
Beef	NA	NA	20.21	29.73	36.70	36.96	25.49	15.00
Sesame	12.70	3.55	5.99	4.06	5.18	4.77	6.38	NA
Tobacco	—	—	.60	.79	1.63	.94	1.08	NA

1. U.S. Dept. of Agriculture figures
2. reflects destruction during civil war

Source: FAO Yearbooks

TABLE NINE

PRICES OF PRINCIPAL EXPORT CROPS (IN DOLLARS PER LB.)

	1978	1979	1980	1981	1982
Cotton	.50	.55	.71	.80	.70
Sugar, raw	.09	.10	.17	.24	.08
Coffee	1.68	1.32	1.67	1.20	1.15
Beef	.90	1.20	1.30	1.17	1.02

Sources: 1978–80, World Bank Report on Nicaragua, 1981; 1981, coffee from USDA, others from Barricada; 1982, Institute for Economic and Social Research (INIES), Managua.

Nicaraguan Political History

1821 Nicaragua and rest of Central America declare independence from Spain and form a federation known as United Provinces of Central America.

1838 The Central American union is dissolved and Nicaragua becomes a republic.

1848 Lake Nicaragua is a major route for prospectors on their way to California Gold Rush. Travel across Nicaragua is under control of a company belonging to Cornelius Vanderbilt.

1850 The United States and Great Britain sign Clayton-Bulwer Treaty, which declares that both nations shall share rights to a trans-Nicaragua Canal. The Nicaraguan government was not consulted.

1855 William Walker and 58 other American adventurers arrive in Nicaragua, having been given free passage on Vanderbilt's ships. Walker declares himself president, reestablishes slavery, and is recognized by U.S. President Pierce.

1857 Walker is defeated by a combined Central American force which fears he will try to impose U.S. rule throughout the area. He takes refuge on a U.S. Navy ship.

1909 President Zalaya resigns in the face of open U.S. hostility after he cancelled U.S. concessions in Nicaragua, borrowed money from Great Britain, and appeared to favor granting Great Britain or Japan rights to a canal across Nicaragua.

1912 U.S. troops arrive to end the political turmoil which followed Zelaya's resignation. They meet armed resistance from a small group organized by Benjamin Zelandon.

1914 Nicaraguan government signs Bryan-Chamorro treaty giving exclusive canal rights to U.S.

1925 Marines leave, feeling incumbent government is sufficiently pro-U.S. and stable.

1926 American troops return as attempts are made to oust pro-U.S. government.

1927 General Moncada, leader of forces opposing incumbent government, agrees to a peace treaty. One of his generals, Augusto César Sandino, rejects peace pact as a perpetuation of U.S.-imposed government. Sandino organizes guerrilla force to oppose American occupation troops.

1933 U.S. troops leave without defeating Sandino. Their role is assumed by the U.S.-created National Guard headed by Anastasio Somoza García.

1934 Sandino is assassinated on orders of Somoza after attending peace talks with President Sacasa.

1936 Somoza forces President Sacasa from office and assumes presidency after fraudulent elections.

1954 Somoza permits Nicaragua to be used as staging area for CIA-sponsored coup against democratically elected Guatemalan President Arbenz.

1956 Somoza is assassinated by poet Rigoberto López Pérez at party celebrating Somoza's "renomination." He is succeeded by his elder son, Luis Somoza.

1961 President Luis Somoza permits Nicaragua to be used as staging area for CIA-sponsored Bay of Pigs Cuba invasion.

1961 Frente Sandinista de Liberación Nacional (FSLN) founded.

1963 Somoza family confidant René Schick assumes presidency. Anastasio Somoza Debayle, brother of Luis, serves as head of National Guard.

1967 Anastasio Somoza Debayle assumes presidency.

1972 Earthquake destroys much of Managua. President Somoza's profiteering from international aid alienates business elite.

1974 FSLN offensive builds momentum after taking hostages at party for Managua's elite and exchanging them for ransom and freedom of political prisoners.

1978 January. Pedro Joaquin Chamorro, editor of opposition *La Prensa*, is assassinated, further isolating Somoza regime.

August. FSLN seizes National Palace, taking dozens of congressmen hostage and exchanging them for ransom, freedom of political prisoners, and safe conduct to Panama.

1979 July 19. FSLN forces triumphantly enter Managua after flight of Somoza.

Sources Consulted

Much of the data for this book was gathered through personal interviews with farmers, ranchers, and farm laborers in Nicaragua; from officials and advisors in the Ministry of Agricultural Development and Agrarian Reform (MIDINRA) and the Ministry of Planning; and from officials and activists of the ATC and UNAG. CIERA, the Center for for Research and Investigation on Agrarian Reform, was my most important single source of information and statistics.

In place of footnotes, I have listed particular sources—many difficult to find outside Nicaragua—used for each chapter; excluded are the hundreds of conversations and informal interviews mentioned above.

Nicaraguan Government Sources

Centro de Investigación y Estudios de la Reforma Agraria (CIERA)

Ministerio de Desarrollo Agropecuario y Reforma Agraria (MIDINRA)

Programa Alimentario Nacional (PAN)

Other Agencies

Fondo Internacional de Desarrollo Agrícola (FIDA)

Food and Agriculture Organization of the United Nations (FAO)

Instituto Centroamericano de Administración de Empresas (INCAE), Managua

International Bank of Reconstruction and Development (IBRD) (World Bank)

TWO—Imagine You Were a Nicaraguan

1. Belli, Pedro, "Growth of Cotton Farming in Nicaragua," Ph.D. dissertation, University of California, Berkeley, 1968.

2. Bendaña, Alejandro, "Crisis in Nicaragua," *NACLA*, 12:6, November–December, 1980.

3. Biderman, Jaime, "Class Structure, the State and Capitalist Development in Nicaraguan Agriculture," Ph.D. dissertation, University of California, Berkeley, 1982.

4. Black, George, *Triumph of the People: The Sandinista Revolution in Nicaragua*, (London: Zed Press, 1981), chapters one through five.

5. Deere, Carmen D. and Marchetti, Peter, "The Worker-Peasant Alliance in the First Year of the Nicaraguan Agrarian Reform," *Latin American Perspectives*, Issue 29, Vol. XIII, No. 2.

6. FAO, *Mission Report: Nicaragua*, October 1979.

7. FAO, Production and Trade Yearbooks.

8. FIDA, *Informe de la Misión Especial de Programación a Nicaragua*, Rome, 1980.

9. IBRD, *The Economic Situation of Nicaragua*, WH–8, August 1953.

10. INCAP/UNASEC/AID Nutrition Sector Assessment (1976), cited in "A Rural Education Program for Nicaragua" by Practical Concepts, Inc., Sept. 17, 1976.

11. INRA, *La Revolución en El Campo*.

12. Korten, Dr. David C., *Crecimiento de la Población y Calidad de la Vida en Nicaragua*, paper prepared for INCAE, 1973.

13. Nuñez, Orlando S., *El Somocismo y El Modelo Capitalista Agro-Exportador*, (Managua: UNAN, 1981).

14. Ryan, John, *Area Handbook for Nicaragua*, (Washington, D.C.: U.S. Printing Office, 1956).

15. Wainker, P. F., "The Agricultural Development of Nicaragua: An Analysis of the Production Sector," Ph.D. dissertation, University of Missouri, 1975.

16. Wheelock, Jaime and Carrion, Luis, "Apuntos Sobre el Desarrollo Económico Político de F.S.L.N., 1980.

17. Wheelock, Jaime, *Imperialismo y Dictadura: Crisis de una Formación Social*, (Mexico, D.F.: Siglo XXI, 1975).

THREE—The Peasants' Victory

1. Black, George, *Triumph of the People: The Sandinista Revolution in Nicaragua*, (London: Zed Press, 1981), chapters six through ten.

2. Dodson, Michael and Montgomery, T. S., "The Churches in the Nicaraguan Revolution," paper presented at the Latin American Studies Association national meeting, Bloomington, Indiana, October 1980.

3. EPICA Task Force, *Nicaragua: A People's Revolution. Part 2*, (Washington: EPICA, 1980).

4. FIDA, *Informe de la Misión Especial de Programación a Nicaragua*, (Rome: 1980).

5. Kaimowitz, David and Thorne, Joseph R., "Nicaragua's Agrarian Reform: The First Year (1979–80)" in Thomas W. Walker, *Nicaragua in Revolution: An Anthology*, (New York: Praeger, 1981).

6. Randall, Margaret, *Sandino's Daughters*, (Vancouver and Toronto: New Star Books, 1981).

7. Selser, Gregory, *Sandino*, (New York: Monthly Review Press, 1981).

FOUR—No Ownership Without Obligation

1. CIERA, *Evaluación de la Política Económica Sandinista en El Sector Agropecuario*, December 1980.

2. *Envio*, Instituto Historico Centroamericano (interview with Xabier Gorostiaga), October 1981.

3. FIDA, *Informe de la Misión Especial de Programación a Nicaragua*, (Rome: 1980).

4. Simon, Laurence, "After the Revolution: An Interview with Jaime Wheelock," *Food Monitor*, July–August 1980.

5. Wheelock, Jaime, speech (Managua), July 14, 1980.

6. Wheelock, Jaime, "No Hay Dos Reformas Iguales," *Nicarauac* (Ministerio de Cultura), Vol. 1, May–June 1980.

FIVE—Failed Partnership: Big Growers and the State

1. *Barricada*, May 30; June 10, 11, 14, 20, 25, 29; July 9, 30, 1981.

2. Black, George, *Triumph of the People: The Sandinista Revolution in Nicaragua*, (London: Zed Press, 1981), chapters eleven, thirteen, and fifteen.

3. *Comercio Exterior*, Banco Nacional de Comercio Exterior, S.A. (Mexico), April 1981.

4. FIDA, *Informe de la Misión Especial de Programación a Nicaragua*, (Rome: 1980).

5. *Envio*, Institute Historico Centroamericano, June 1981.

6. *Latin America Regional Reports: Mexico & Central America*, RM–81–07, Aug. 14, 1981.

7. Ministerio de Desarrollo Agropecuario y Reforma Agraria, *Tres Años de Reforma Agraria*, May 4, 1982.

8. *Nuevo Diario*, July 4, 1981.

9. *Proceso* (Mexico), July 20, 1981.

SIX—Spilling Credit in the Countryside

1. CIERA, *Datas Generales Sobre El Sector Campesino*, April 1982.

2. CIERA, *La Pequeña Producción: Estudios de Casas*, July 1980.

3. Deere, Carmen D. and Marchetti, Peter, "The Worker-Peasant Alliance in the First Year of the Nicaraguan Agrarian Reform," *Latin American Perspectives*, Issue 29, Vol. XIII, No. 2.

4. FIDA, *Informe de la Misión Especial de Programación a Nicaragua*, (Rome: 1980).

5. Marchetti, Peter, "Reforma Agraria y La Conversión Difícil: Republicación de Recursos, Redistribución de Poder, y Los Explotados del Campo en Chile y en Nicaragua," *Estudios Rurales Latin Americas*, Vol. 4, No.

SEVEN—The State Farm: Discredited Model or Pragmatic Adaptation?

1. CIERA, *Informes Sobre Las Empresas de Servicios del Estado*, June 1980; *Informe para El Segundo Aniversario*, June 1981; *Informe del Ministerio de Desarrollo Agropecuario*, August 1980.

2. Deere, Carmen D. and Marchetti, Peter, "The Worker-Peasant Alliance in the First Year of the Nicaraguan Agrarian Reform," *Latin American Perspectives*, Issue 29, Vol. XIII, No. 2.

3. *Envio*, Institute Historico Centroamericano, March 15, 1982.

4. FIDA, *Informe de la Misión Especial de Programación a Nicaragua*, (Rome: 1980).

5. Franco, Brother Luis, "The First Steps of the Nicaraguan Agrarian Reform in León: An Interview by Michael Scott, Oxfam-America," Nov. 5, 1980.

6. INCAE, *Altamira: Empresa Lechera del Pueblo Roger Deshon Arguello* and *Complejo Azucarero Julio Buitrago*.

7. Ministerio de Desarrollo Agropecuario y Reforma Agraria, *Tres Años de Reforma Agraria*, May 5, 1982.

8. Wheelock, Jaime, "No Hay Dos Reformas Iguales," *Nicarauac* (Ministerio de Cultura), Vol. 1, May–June 1980.

EIGHT—Wage and Productivity Dilemmas

1. *Barricada*, April 28, 30, 1980; May 8, 14, 17, 1980.

2. Black, George, *Triumph of the People: The Sandinista Revolution in Nicaragua*, (London: Zed Press, 1981), chapter thirteen.

3. CIERA, *Informes Sobre Las Empresas de Servicios del Estado*, June 1980; *Informe para El Segundo Aniversario*, June 1981; *Informe del Ministerio de Desarrollo Agropecuario*, Aug. 1980.

4. FIDA, *Informe de la Misión Especial de Programación a Nicaragua*, (Rome: 1980).

5. *El Machete* (Associación de Trabajadores del Campo—ATC), February 1980.

6. INCAE, *Altamira: Empresa Lechera del Pueblo Roger Deshon Arguello* and *Complejo Azucarero Julio Buitrago*.

7. *Poder Sandinista* (Secretaria Nacional de Propaganda y Educación Politica del F.S.L.N.), Sept. 12, 1980.

NINE—Is Seizing the Land Revolutionary?

1. *Barricada*, Feb. 16, 17, 1981.
2. Black, George, *Triumph of the People: The Sandinista Revolution in Nicaragua*, (London: Zed Press, 1981), chapters one through five.
3. FIDA, *Informe de la Misión Especial de Programación a Nicaragua*, (Rome: 1980).
4. *Intercontinental Press*, March 3, 1981.
5. Wheelock, Jaime, "No Hay Dos Reformas Iguales," *Nicarauac* (Ministerio de Cultura), Vol. 1, May–June 1980.

TEN—A Conservative Agrarian Reform?

1. *Central American Report*, Vol. IX, No. 25, July 2, 1982, pp. 199f.
2. *Envio*, Institute Historico Centroamericano, Aug. 1981.
3. Kaimowitz, David and Thorne, Joseph R., "Nicaragua's Agrarian Reform: The First Year (1979–80)" in Thomas W. Walker, *Nicaragua in Revolution: An Anthology*, (New York: Praeger, 1981).
4. *La Gaceta* (diario oficial), Managua, Aug. 21, 1981; Oct. 2, 1981.
5. Marchetti, Peter, interview in *Now We Can Speak*, Lappé and Collins, (San Francisco: Institute for Food and Development Policy, 1982).
6. Marchetti, Peter, interview in *Working Papers*, March–April 1982.
7. Mayorga, Salvador, interview in *Now We Can Speak*.
8. Ministerio de Desarrollo Agropecuario y Reforma Agraria, *Tres Años de Reforma Agraria*, May 4, 1982.

ELEVEN—Cooperative Work: Will It Work in Nicaragua?

1. CIERA, *Datas Generales Sobre El Sector Campesino*, April 1982.
2. CIERA, *Evaluación de la Política Económica Sandinista en El Sector Agropecuario*, December 1980.
3. FIDA, *Informe de la Misión Especial de Programación a Nicaragua*, (Rome: 1980).

4. Marchetti, Peter, "Reforma Agraria y La Conversión Difícil: Republicación de Recursos, Redistribución de Poder, y Los Explotados del Campo en Chile y en Nicaragua," *Estudios Rurales Latin Americas*, Vol. 4, No.

TWELVE—Corns and Beans First

1. Comisión de Propaganda Agropecuaria, *Propaganda del PAN*.

2. FIDA, *Informe de la Misión Especial de Programación a Nicaragua*, (Rome: 1980).

3. George, Susan, *Prospects for Nicaraguan Exports of Basic Grains in the Present World Agricultural and Political Context*, Report to INRA-CIERA, March 18, 1981.

4. Ministerio de Desarrollo Agropecuario y Reforma Agraria, *Tres Años de Reforma Agraria*, May 4, 1982.

5. *Nuevo Diario*, "Defensa del Consumidor" (special page appearing every Wednesday).

6. PAN, *Programa Alimentario Nacional*, May 1981.

7. Barraclough, Solon and Marchetti, Peter (United Nations Research Institute for Social Development and CIERA), *A Preliminary Analysis of the Nicaraguan Food System*, (Geneva and Managua: June 1982).

8. Vergapopoulos, Kostas, "L'Agriculture Pérepherique dans le Nouvel Order International," paper delivered at the Fifth World Congress of Rural Sociology, Mexico, D.F., August 1980.

THIRTEEN—Can the Market Feed the Poor?

1. *Barricada*, June 2, 4, 5, 15, 1980.

2. CIERA, "Managua Food System Study: Preliminary Report."

3. FIDA, *Informe de la Misión Especial de Programación a Nicaragua*, (Rome: 1980).

4. Ministerio de Planificación, *Determinación y Análisis de la Satisfacción de las Necesidades Básicas en Los Sectores Urbanos de Nicaragua*, May 1981.

5. *Nuevo Diario*, July 1, 1981.

6. *Nuevo Diario*, "Defensa del Consumidor" (special page appearing every Wednesday).

7. PAN, *Programa Proletario de la Revolución*, May 1981.

Nicaragua Resource Guide

Books

1. Aleman, Luis; Cendales, Lola; Marino, German; McFadden, John; Peresson, Mario; Suarez, Maria; and Tamez, Carlos; *Vencimos: La Cruzada Nacional de Alfabetización de Nicaragua: Libro Abierto Para America Latina*, International Development Research Centre, Box 8500, Ottawa, Ontario, Canada K1G 3H9. Definitive work on the Nicaraguan literacy campaign written by participants in the effort. In Spanish only.

2. Bevan, John and Black, George, *The Loss of Fear: Education in Nicaragua Before and After the Revolution*. From National Solidarity Campaign, 20 Compton Terrace, London N1.

3. Black, George, *Triumph of the People—The Sandinista Revolution in Nicaragua*, Zed Press (London). Excellent and thorough resource. $7.95 plus $1.50 postage from National Network in Solidarity with the Nicaraguan People (NNSNP), 930 F St. NW, #720, Washington, DC 20004, (202) 223-2328.

4. Cardenal, Ernesto, *The Gospel in Solentiname*, Orbis Books (Maryknoll, New York), 1976.

5. Cardenal, Ernesto, *Zero Hour and Other Documentary Poems*, New Direction Books (New York), 1980.

6. EPICA Task Force, *Nicaragua: A People's Revolution*. 100-page primer. $4.25 plus $.75 postage from EPICA, 1470 Irving Street NW, Washington, DC 20010.

7. Hinde, Peter, *Look! A New Thing in the Americas*. A Carmelite priest looks at the role of the church in Nicaragua. $1.00, available in bulk from National Network.

8. Lappé, Frances Moore and Collins, Joseph, *Now We Can Speak: A Journey through the New Nicaragua*, Institute for Food and Development Policy (San Francisco), 1982. Interviews with many Nicaraguans. $4.95 from IFDP, 1885 Mission Street, San Francisco, CA 94103.

9. Meiselas, Susan, *Nicaragua June '78-July '79*, Pantheon Books (New York), 1981. Color photographs and chronology. $11.95.

10. Millet, Richard, *Guardians of the Dynasty: A History of the U.S.-Created Guardia National de Nicaragua and the Somoza Family*, Orbis Books (Maryknoll, New York), 1977.

11. Randall, Margaret, *Sandino's Daughters*, New Star Books (Vancouver and Toronto), 1981. From the Crossing Press, Trumansberg, NY 14886.

12. Selser, Gregorio, *Sandino*, Monthly Review Press (New York), 1981.

13. Walker, Thomas, *Nicaragua in Revolution: An Anthology*, Praeger (New York), 1981.

14. Weber, Henri, *Nicaragua: The Sandinist Revolution*, New Left Review Editions (London), 1981.

15. Wheelock, Jaime, *Imperialismo y Dictadura*, Siglo XXI (Mexico City), 3rd edition, 1979.

Articles and Pamphlets

1. Cardenal, Fernando and Miller, Valerie, "Nicaragua 1980: The Battle of the ABC's," *Harvard Educational Review*, vol. 50, no. 1, February 1981, pp. 1-19. Reprint $1 from 13 Appian Way, Cambridge, MA 02138.

2. Council on Interracial Books for Children, "The Literacy Crusade in Nicaragua," *Interracial Books for Children*, vol. 12, no. 2, 1981. Reprint $1 from CIBC, 1841 Broadway, New York, NY 10023.

3. Landis, Fred, "CIA Psychological Warfare Operations: How the CIA Manipulates the Media in Nicaragua, Chile, and Jamaica," *Science for the People*, vol. 14, no. 1, Jan/Feb 1982. Available from Science for the People, 897 Main Street, Cambridge, MA 02139.

4. "New Fact Sheets on Nicaragua." Fact sheets on Destabilization, Government and Mass Politics, Women, Atlantic Coast, Agrarian Reform, and Church. From National Network.

5. North American Congress on Latin America, *Target Nicaragua*. Special January-February 1982 issue on destabilization, counter-revolution, the Atlantic Coast, and U.S. maneuvers in the region. $3.75 postpaid from NACLA, 151 West 19th Street, 9th Floor, New York, NY 10011.

6. Trueman, Beverly, "Nicaragua's Second Revolution" and "1984: 'The Revolution is Not a Piñata,'" *Christianity and Crisis*, vol. 41, no. 17, Nov. 2, 1981. $1 from Christianity and Crisis, 537 West 121st Street, New York, NY 10027.

Periodicals

1. *Envio*, monthly "letter" on political, economic, and social developments in Nicaragua from the Jesuit-run Instituto Historico de Centroamerica. Very useful. Available in English from Central American Historical Institute, Intercultural Center, Georgetown University, Washington D.C. 20057 for $25 per year. Available in Spanish or German from Apartado A–194, Managua, Nicaragua.

2. *NACLA Report on the Americas*, bimonthly, NACLA, 151 West 19th Street, New York, NY 10011. $15 per year.

3. *Nicaragua*, bimonthly, National Network, address above. $5.00 per year, U.S.; $8.00, Mexico/Canada; $10.00 elsewhere.

4. *Nicaragua Update*, bimonthly, Nicaragua Interfaith Committee for Action (NICA), 942 Market Street, Room 709, San Francisco, CA 94102, (415) 433-6057. $7.00.

5. *Nicaraguan Perspectives*, quarterly, Nicaragua Information Center, P. O. Box 1004, Berkeley, CA 94704, (415) 549-1387. $10 per year.

6. *WOLA Update*, bimonthly plus special reports, Washington Office on Latin America, 110 Maryland Avenue NE, Washington, DC 20002. $10.00 per year.

Films

1. *From the Ashes*, 16mm, color, 60 min, English subtitles, available from Document Associates, 211 E. 43rd Street, New York, NY 10017, (212) 682-0730. The reconstruction of Nicaragua from the point of view of one family.

2. *Sandino Hoy y Siempre*, 16mm, color, 57 min, English subtitles, available from Icarus Films, 200 Park Avenue South, Suite

1319, New York, NY 10003. A portrait of Nicaragua and its people during the reconstruction process.

3. *Sandino Vive!*, 16mm, color, 28 min, 1980, Spanish or English, free loan from Maryknoll, Maryknoll, NY. The church's role in the overthrow of Somoza.

4. *Thanks to God and the Revolution*, 16mm, color, 30 min, English subtitles, available from Icarus Films. An inquiry into the role of Christians in social change and armed struggle.

5. *These Same Hands (Nicaragua: Las Mismas Manos)*, 3/4-inch videocassette format, 53 min, available from World Focus Films, 2125 Russell Street, Berkeley, CA 94705, (415) 848-8126. $50 rental, $250 purchase (no 16mm·version).

6. *The Uprising*, 35mm, color, 96 min, Spanish or English, available from Kino International, 250 West 57th Street, New York, NY 10019, (212) 586-8720. Director Peter Lilienthal's dramatization of events during the final period of fighting in 1979.

7. *Women in Arms*, 16mm, color, 59 min, Spanish or English, available from Hudson River Productions, P. O. Box 515, Franklin Lakes, NJ 07417. Participation of women in the war and the transformation of society.

Tape and Slide Shows

1. "Central America: Roots of the Crisis," 27 min, 131 slides, available from American Friends Service Committee, Latin American Program, 1501 Cherry Street, Philadelphia, PA 19102, (215) 241-7159. $50 purchase, $15 one-week rental. (Revised and updated, August 1981.) A look at the history, economics, and politics of the current situation in the region.

2. "Nicaragua: The Challenge of Revolution," 25 min, 139 slides/tape presentation with script and information packet, available from NNSNP, $15.00 rental. Describes the most important developments in the revolutionary process.

3. "Nicaragua Libre," 20 min, 80 b/w slides, available from Jeanne Gallo, SND, 24 Curtis Avenue, Somerville, MA 02144, $65 purchase. Social conditions and history of struggle plus the effort to build a new society.

4. "Now We're Awakened! Women in Nicaragua," 30 min, 80 color slides/tape and information packet, $15 rental from NNSNP, $75 purchase from PAN, 410 Merritt 7, Oakland, CA

94610. Women's participation in the overthrow of the dictatorship and the building of a new order in Nicaragua.

Organizations

1. National Network in Solidarity with the Nicaraguan People
   (NNSNP), 930 F Street NW #720, Washington, DC 20004,
   (202) 223-2328 or 626-9598.

2. Nicaragua Interfaith Committee for Action (NICA), 942
   Market Street, Room 709, San Francisco, CA 94102, (415)
   433-6057.

3. North American Congress on Latin America (NACLA), 151
   West 19th Street, New York, NY 10011 (212) 989-8890.

4. Washington Office on Latin America (WOLA), 110 Maryland
   Avenue NE, Washington, DC 20002 (202) 544-8045.

5. Institute for Food and Development Policy (IFDP), 1885 Mission Street, San Francisco, CA 94103, (415) 864-8555.

Institute Publications

Now We Can Speak: A Journey through the New Nicaragua, features interviews with Nicaraguans from every walk of life telling how their lives have changed since the 1979 overthrow of the Somoza dictatorship. Frances Moore Lappé and Joseph Collins, 124 pages. $4.95

Diet for a Small Planet: Tenth Anniversary Edition, an updated edition of the bestseller that taught Americans the social and personal significance of a new way of eating. Frances Moore Lappé, 432 pages with charts, tables, resource guide, recipes, Ballantine Books. $3.50

Development Debacle: The World Bank in the Philippines, uses the World Bank's own secret documents to show how its ambitious development plans actually hurt the very people they were supposed to aid—the poor majority. Walden Bello, David Kinley, and Elaine Elinson, 270 pages with bibliography and tables. $6.95

Food First Comic, a comic for young people based on the book *Food First: Beyond the Myth of Scarcity*. Leonard Rifas, 24 pages. $1.00

Trading the Future: How Booming Farm Exports Threaten Our Food Security traces the worldwide shift from food self-sufficiency to export dependence and shows how U.S. grain exports accelerate this trend. James Wessel, with Frances Moore Lappé and Mort Hantman, 150 pages. Available May 1983. $4.95 (est.)

Seeds of the Earth: A Private or Public Resource? examines the rapid erosion of the earth's gene pool of seed varieties and the control of the seed industry by multinational corporations. Pat Roy Mooney, 126 pages with tables and corporate profiles. $7.00

World Hunger: Ten Myths clears the way for each of us to work in appropriate ways to end needless hunger. Frances Moore Lappé and Joseph Collins, revised and updated, 72 pages with photographs. $2.95

El Hambre en el Mundo: Diez Mitos, a Spanish-language version of *World Hunger: Ten Myths* plus additional information about food and agriculture policies in Mexico, 72 pages.
$1.45

Food First: Beyond the Myth of Scarcity, 50 questions and responses about the causes and proposed remedies for world hunger. Frances Moore Lappé and Joseph Collins, with Cary Fowler, 620 pages, Ballantine Books, revised 1979. $3.95

Food First Resource Guide, documentation on the roots of world hunger and rural poverty. Institute staff, 80 pages with photographs. $3.00

Aid as Obstacle: Twenty Questions about our Foreign Aid and the Hungry demonstrates that foreign aid may be hurting the very people we want to help and explains why foreign aid programs fail. Frances Moore Lappé, Joseph Collins, David Kinley, 192 pages with photographs. $4.95

Needless Hunger: Voices from a Bangladesh Village exposes the often brutal political and economic roots of needless hunger. Betsy Hartmann and James Boyce, 72 pages with photographs. $3.50

What Can We Do? An action guide on food, land and hunger issues. Interviews with over one dozen North Americans involved in many aspects of these issues. William Valentine and Frances Moore Lappé, 60 pages with photographs. $2.95

Mozambique and Tanzania: Asking the Big Questions looks at the questions which face people working to build economic and political systems based on equity, participation, and cooperation. Frances Moore Lappé and Adele Bec-car-Varela, 126 pages with photographs. $4.75

Circle of Poison documents a scandal of global propor-tions, the export of dangerous pesticides to Third World countries. David Weir and Mark Schapiro, 101 pages with photos and tables. $3.95

Casting New Molds: First Steps towards Worker Control in a Mozambique Steel Factory, a personal account of the day-to-day struggle of Mozambique workers by Peter Sketch-ley, with Frances Moore Lappé, 64 pages. $3.95

Agrarian Reform and Counter-Reform in Chile, a first-hand look at some of the current economic policies in Chile and their effect on the rural majority. Joseph Collins, 24 pages with photographs. $1.45

Research Reports. "Land Reform: Is It the Answer? A Venezuelan Peasant Speaks." Frances Moore Lappé and Hannes Lorenzen, 17 pages. $1.50

"Export Agriculture: An Energy Drain." Mort Hantman, 50 pages. $3.00

Seeds of Revolution is a provocative documentary about hunger, land reform, multinational agribusiness, and the military in Honduras. Produced by Howard Enders for ABC News, with the assistance of Joseph Collins, 30 minutes, 16mm color. $450 purchase, $50 rental

Food First Slideshow/Filmstrip in a visually positive and powerful portrayal demonstrates that the cause of hunger is not scarcity but the increasing concentration of control over food producing resources, 30 minutes.

$89 (slideshow), $34 (filmstrip)

Write for our free publications catalogue.

All publications orders must be prepaid.

Institute for Food and Development Policy
1885 Mission Street
San Francisco, CA 94103 USA
(415) 864-8555

About the Institute

The Institute for Food and Development Policy, also known as Food First, is a not-for-profit public education center. Founded in 1975 by Frances Moore Lappé and Joseph Collins, the Institute focuses on food and agriculture, always asking: Why hunger in a world of plenty?

By working to identify the root causes of hunger and food problems here and abroad, the Institute provides counter-messages:

—No country in the world is a hopeless basket case.

—The illusion of scarcity is a product of the unequal control over food-producing resources; inequality in control over these resources results in their underuse and misuse.

—The hungry are not our enemies. Rather, we and they are victims of the same economic forces which are undercutting their food security as well as ours.

Financial Support
The Institute solicits contributions from individuals, church groups, and private foundations. More and more, it depends on individual contributions, the sale of Institute publications, and speaking honoraria.

We are especially grateful to have the continuing support of the many Institute Sustainers and Friends of the Institute.

In addition to this broad base of international support, we want to thank current foundation and individual supporters. (Financial support does not necessarily reflect agreement with the views expressed in Institute publications.)

Friends of the Institute
Because the Institute's work threatens many established interests, we believe that our effectiveness depends on developing the widest possible base of support. By joining the Friends of the Institute program you can receive our expanding list of publications at a generous discount or free, while contributing in a fundamental way to the ongoing work of the Institute.

All contributors of $25 or more receive a free copy of the paperback edition of the highly acclaimed *Food First: Beyond the Myth of Scarcity* by Frances Moore Lappé and Joseph Collins with Cary Fowler (Ballantine, 1979). Contributors of $100 or more also receive one free copy of all major Institute publications for one year. Contributors of $25 or more also receive a 50 percent discount on one copy of all Institute publications for one year.

All contributions are tax-deductible.

Dear Food First,
( ) *Yes, I support the kind of work you are doing—such as this book on Nicaragua. I'd like to become a Friend of the Institute.*
( ) *Please send me more information about the Institute, including your publications catalog.*
(Mail to IFDP, 1885 Mission St., San Francisco CA 94103 USA.)

*Name*_____

*Address*_____

*City/State/Zip/Country*_____

*Telephone*_____